D1278185

Writing the Critical Essay

Prisons

An OPPOSING VIEWPOINTS® Guide

Jamuna Carroll, *Book Editor*

Christine Nasso, *Publisher*
Elizabeth Des Chenes, *Managing Editor*

OPPOSING
VIEWPOINTS®
SERIES

GREENHAVEN PRESS
An imprint of Thomson Gale, a part of The Thomson Corporation

THOMSON
GALE

Detroit • New York • San Francisco • New Haven, Conn. • Waterville, Maine • London

LIBRARY OF CONGRESS CATALOGING-IN-PUBLICATION DATA

Prisons / Jamuna Carroll, book editor.
   p. cm. — (Writing the critical essay)
  Includes bibliographical references and index.
  ISBN-13: 978-0-7377-3584-0 (hardcover : alk. paper)
  ISBN-10: 0-7377-3584-8 (hardcover : alk. paper)
  1. Prisons. 2. Crime prevention. 3. Essay—Authorship. 4. Written communication—Study and teaching. I. Carroll, Jamuna.
  HV8491.P77 2006
  365—dc22
          2006031176

Printed in the United States of America

CONTENTS

9000964414

Examining the state of writing and how it is taught in the United States was the official purpose of the National Commission on Writing in America's Schools and Colleges. The commission, made up of teachers, school administrators, business leaders, and college and university presidents, released its first report in 2003. "Despite the best efforts of many educators," commissioners argued, "writing has not received the full attention it deserves." Among the findings of the commission was that most fourth-grade students spent less than three hours a week writing, that three-quarters of high school seniors never receive a writing assignment in their history or social studies classes, and that more than 50 percent of first-year students in college have problems writing error-free papers. The commission called for a "cultural sea change" that would increase the emphasis on writing for both elementary and secondary schools. These conclusions have made some educators realize that writing must be emphasized in the curriculum. As colleges are demanding an ever-higher level of writing proficiency from incoming students, schools must respond by making students more competent writers. In response to these concerns, the SAT, an influential standardized test used for college admissions, required an essay for the first time in 2005.

Books in the Writing the Critical Essay: An Opposing Viewpoints Guide series use the patented Opposing Viewpoints format to help students learn to organize ideas and arguments and to write essays using common critical writing techniques. Each book in the series focuses on a particular type of essay writing—including expository, persuasive, descriptive, and narrative—that students learn while being taught both the five-paragraph essay as well as longer pieces of writing that have an opinionated focus. These guides include everything necessary to help students research, outline, draft, edit, and ultimately write successful essays across the curriculum, including essays for the SAT.

Using Opposing Viewpoints

This series is inspired by and builds upon Greenhaven Press's acclaimed Opposing Viewpoints series. As in the parent series, each book in the Writing the Critical Essay series focuses on a timely and controversial social issue that provides lots of opportunities for creating thought-provoking essays. The first section of each volume begins with a brief introductory essay that provides context for the opposing viewpoints that follow. These articles are chosen for their accessibility and clearly stated views. The thesis of each article is made explicit in the article's title and is accentuated by its pairing with an opposing or alternative view. These essays are both models of persuasive writing techniques and valuable research material that students can mine to write their own informed essays. Guided reading and discussion questions help lead students to key ideas and writing techniques presented in the selections.

The second section of each book begins with a preface discussing the format of the essays and examining characteristics of the featured essay type. Model five-paragraph and longer essays then demonstrate that essay type. The essays are annotated so that key writing elements and techniques are pointed out to the student. Sequential, step-by-step exercises help students construct and refine thesis statements; organize material into outlines; analyze and try out writing techniques; write transitions, introductions, and conclusions; and incorporate quotations and other researched material. Ultimately, students construct their own compositions using the designated essay type.

The third section of each volume provides additional research material and writing prompts to help the student. Additional facts about the topic of the book serve as a convenient source of supporting material for essays. Other features help students go beyond the book for their research. Like other Greenhaven Press books, each book in the Writing the Critical Essay series includes bibliographic listings of relevant periodical articles, books, Web sites, and organizations to contact.

Writing the Critical Essay: An Opposing Viewpoints Guide will help students master essay techniques that can be used in any discipline.

Background to Controversy: America's Prisoners: Forgotten Citizens

T he United States has more people in prison than any other industrialized nation. Locked away for crimes as minor as not paying traffic tickets to those as heinous as multiple murder, prisoners' treatment and well-being is rarely thought of once they are placed in prisons. Unfortunately, because many of these prisoners will be allowed to rejoin society, the fact that they are forgotten can mean that they are little more than warehoused. Many return to prison again, unable to cope with the outside world.

The issue of prisoners' forgotten status was thrust into the spotlight after Hurricane Katrina, the violent storm that devastated the southern coast of The United States in August 2005. As water flooded New Orleans, the Orleans Parish Prison, one of the oldest buildings in the city, was plunged into chaos. When the prison lost power, guards fled the building. Prisoners became trapped in the prison in sweltering heat. They were without supplies, unable to leave their cells, and had no information about what was happening in the city around them. According to a report on the prison published by the American Civil Liberties Union in August 2006, "Deputies left their posts whole-sale, leaving behind prisoners in locked cells, some standing in sewage-tainted water up to their chests. Over the next few days, without food, water, or ventilation, prisoners broke windows in order to get air, and carved holes in the jail's walls in an effort to get to safety."[1]

The prisoners were evacuated by state officials after three days, but spent the following weeks being transferred to jails and prisons around Louisiana, many of which had

Prisoners are evacuated from Orleans Parish Prison after Hurricane Katrina. Among other social problems, Katrina shed light on the issue of how America treats its prisoners.

been damaged by the storm as well. Those who were transferred to the Elayn Hunt Correctional Center in St. Gabriel, Louisiana, for example, were placed outdoors in a yard with little food and poor medical care. Because the prisoners were crowded all together, many armed themselves with makeshift weapons, causing further chaos and violence.

In the aftermath of the hurricane, the Department of Corrections lost track of the prisoners, their crimes, and their sentences. The extensive flooding and devastation had destroyed many city records, and hundreds of prisoners became lost in the system. Some prisoners, incarcerated for minor offenses, were unable to prove that they were scheduled for release.

For example, Ivy Gisclair was being held at the Orleans Parish Prison when Katrina struck. He was serving a two month sentence for owing $700 in unpaid parking tickets and other minor traffic violations, and had no previous record. After being trapped in the Orleans Parish Prison, Gisclair was transferred to two different prisons and became lost in the system. When he tried to tell guards that his release date had passed, Gisclair claims, he was severely beaten by the prison guards and kept in his cell. Gisclair was finally released from prison when his mother faxed his court documents to the prison, which proved he had been held more than a month after his scheduled release date. According to National Public Radio reporter Ari Shapiro, "If his mother hadn't been around, or if his records had been destroyed in the storm, he might still be in prison today."[2]

New Orleans prisoners are transferred to temporary prisons after Hurricane Katrina. Amid post-Katrina chaos, authorities lost track of several prisoners.

The plight of Gisclair and other inmates who endured the chaos following Hurricane Katrina underscored for some the need for even the worst members of society to be accorded their rights. "The prisoners inside the Orleans Parish Prison suffered some of the worst horrors of Hurricane

Katrina," said Eric Balaban, an attorney for the National Prison Project. "Because society views prisoners as second-class citizens, their stories have largely gone unnoticed and therefore untold."[3]

Although Gisclair was released, hundreds of other inmates are still held on questionable charges or in violation of their sentences as a result of Louisiana's ailing system. Though nearly everyone associated with the New Orleans justice and correctional systems agree that they have a problem on their hands, officials are split about how to handle it. Some, such as Criminal Court judge Arthur Hunter, believe that inmates should be let out of prison until their crimes and charges can be sorted out. In fact, Hunter has vowed to use his courtroom for this purpose, keeping within the confines of the law. Pamela Metzger, a Tulane law professor who has spearheaded a project with her law students to extricate prisoners from the confusion, agrees with Hunter. "It is profoundly dishonorable to know that poor people are lost in the system without lawyers and that they are in jail because [the dis-

Released from jail by judicial order, Dyan French (left) speaks with an official of the Orleans Parish district attorney's office. French had been arrested before Katrina, but never charged with a crime.

trict attorney's] office has charged them with a crime, and [is doing] nothing to facilitate making sure that that person has their constitutional rights,"[4] said Metzger.

Other officials, such as New Orleans district attorney Eddie Jordan, argue that some inmates are dangerous criminals and therefore should not be released until their identity can be confirmed. "The fact that they're in jail today I think is a strong indication that they need to stay in jail until they have their day in court,"[5] said Jordan. Similarly, former Louisiana attorney general Richard Ieyoub advocates releasing minor offenders, but warns against mistakenly freeing violent and dangerous criminals in the process.

Thinking about and delving into America's forgotten citizens is the subject of this book. Writing the Critical Essay: an Opposing Viewpoints Guide: *Prisons* exposes readers to the basic arguments made about prisons and encourages them to develop their own opinions on whether or not prisons are useful or harmful, should be used to punish or rehabilitate, and cultivate or curb violence. Through skill-building exercises and thoughtful discussion questions, students will articulate their own thoughts about prisons and develop tools to craft their own essays on the subject.

Notes

1. "Abandoned & Abused: Orleans Parish Prisoners in the Wake of Hurricane Katrina," American Civil Liberties Union, August 10, 2006, p. 9.

2. Ari Shapiro, "Judge Vows to Free Inmates Held Since Katrina Hit," *National Public Radio, Morning Edition,* August 25, 2005. www.npr.org/templates/story/story. php?storyId=5708448.

3. Quoted in "The People Who Were Left to Die," *San Francisco Bay View,* August 19, 2006.

4. Quoted in Shapiro, "Judge Vows to Free Inmates Held Since Katrina Hit."

5. Quoted in Shapiro, "Judge Vows to Free Inmates Held Since Katrina Hit."

**Section One:
Opposing
Viewpoints
on Prisons**

Prisons Reduce Crime

David Muhlhausen

In the following article David Muhlhausen argues that crime was reduced significantly in America after the country began jailing more lawbreakers. Research shows that seventeen offenses are prevented for every offender who is locked up, Muhlhausen notes. Therefore, he concludes, the high incarceration rate today keeps millions of people from becoming victims of crime. He recommends building more prisons in order to sustain the low crime rate.

Muhlhausen is a senior research analyst at the Heritage Foundation's Center for Data Analysis. The Heritage Foundation is a conservative research institute.

Consider the following questions:

1. In Muhlhausen's opinion, what will happen if leniency is offered to offenders who do not deserve it?
2. What percentage of states' operational budgets is set aside for corrections, according to the author?
3. In Muhlhausen's view, what is the government's first and foremost job?

Signs can be found nationwide that what critics call America's "love affair" with incarcerating prisoners may be coming to an end.

America Relies on the Criminal Justice System

The legislature of Washington state, which passed the nation's first three-strikes-you're-out law by popular initiative [in 1994], recently passed a series of laws weakening it. Kansas now orders first-time drug offenders to treatment rather than prison, provided they didn't commit a crime that involved violence. Michigan has dropped its lengthy mandatory-minimum sentences for drug offenders. Iowa, Missouri and Wisconsin have eased their "truth in sentencing" laws, which require inmates to serve nearly their entire sentences before being eligible for parole.

In the last year, 25 states have sought to reduce the burden on their budgets and their corrections systems by weakening mandatory-sentencing statutes, reforming post-release requirements and restoring parole. Those proposing these measures come from both sides of the political aisle and from every level of government. They include sheriffs and police chiefs, legisla-

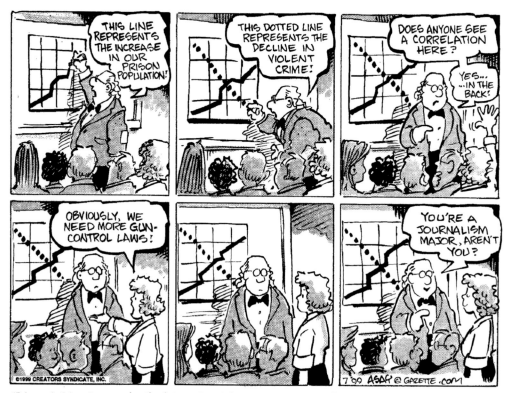

"Prisons & Crime," cartoon by Chuck Asay. Copyright © 1999 Creators Syndicate. Reproduced by permission of Chuck Asay and Creators Syndicate, Inc.

tors and members of Congress, governors and prison executives.

But if Alan Elsner, an author who focuses on criminal-justice issues, was correct in a recent op-ed for *The Washington Post* that our "love affair" with incarcerating dangerous criminals is waning, those proposing the changes are going to find that breaking up is hard to do. Americans have come to rely on the criminal-justice system to keep hard-core offenders locked up, and they won't think it's worth it when—in the name of cost-cutting—rapes, murders and other violent crimes go up by the thousands as a result of any veiled efforts to extend leniency to offenders who clearly don't deserve it.

Incarceration Prevents Crime

The American people understand their state governments are in financial crisis and that the federal government expects record deficits in the near future. They sense that locking up some prisoners—first-time drug offenders, for instance—may be draining state money needlessly. The increased emphasis on rehabilitating prisoners and easing their return to society that President [George W.] Bush advocated in his recent [2004] State of the Union speech makes sense to many of them.

But they also know that the strengthening of sentencing laws in the early 1990s, the prison-building boom that began in that decade and efforts by prosecutors and lawmakers to take dangerous criminals off the street and keep them off has paid handsome dividends.

The prison population in America has quadrupled since 1980 to more than 2 million people. Crime rates during the decade dropped to all-time lows. Coincidence? Consider that researchers have found that 15 crimes are committed for every person released from prison, and that 17 crimes are avoided for every person put into prison. Also along those lines, a 10 percent increase in prison population leads to a 13 percent decrease in homicides.

Considering that half the people in America's prisons are serving time for violent crimes, that means that, conservatively, millions of people have avoided becoming victims of such crimes thanks to these policies.

So pardon them if they're not quick to slash corrections budgets when corrections makes up so small a part of states' operational expenditures—about 6.7 percent, according to the latest research. Pardon their skepticism of a rehabilitation system with a long, miserable record of failure—two-thirds of those released from prison this year will be re-arrested within three years and almost 49 percent of the violent criminals released will return to prison in that time period.

The Government Needs to Take Prisons Seriously

There is a lot of discussion in the country these days about the proper role and size of government. But all agree that providing for the public safety is its first and foremost job.

Right now, that means operating and building prisons will remain for some time to come a significant priority of government. America's state prisons operate today at up to 117 percent capacity, which means two things: we must ensure we incarcerate only those who truly should be in prison, and we must face the fact that we need more prisons, not fewer.

States can save money by more effectively prioritizing within their criminal-justice systems. They can find alternatives for first-time drug offenders and others who haven't committed violent crimes. They can bolster vocational training, which shows some promise of better preparing prisoners to find employment after release.

We Need More Prisons

But there's only so much that can be done. America faced a real problem when the prison-building and sentence-strengthening movements began—a wave of violent crime that left much of the nation gripped in fear. This problem got better in the 1990s, but it hasn't gone away. And even if we can decrease recidivism, those who commit crimes,

Imprisonable Offenses

Since 1995, more than half of the increase in State prison populations is accounted for by those convicted of violent crimes.

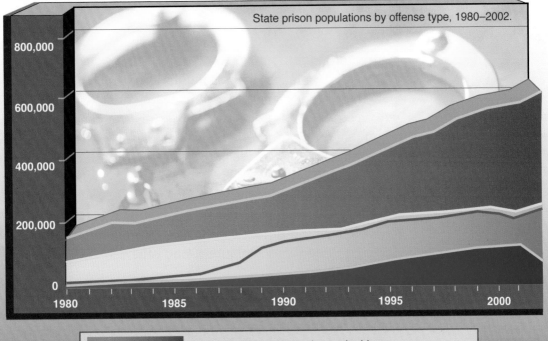

State prison populations by offense type, 1980–2002.

800,000

600,000

400,000

200,000

0

1980   1985   1990   1995   2000

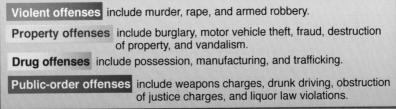

Violent offenses include murder, rape, and armed robbery.

Property offenses include burglary, motor vehicle theft, fraud, destruction of property, and vandalism.

Drug offenses include possession, manufacturing, and trafficking.

Public-order offenses include weapons charges, drunk driving, obstruction of justice charges, and liquor law violations.

Source: Bureau of Justice Statistics, www.ojp.usdoj.gov/bjs.

especially violent crimes, owe a debt to society and need to do their time.

In truth, America does not love prisons. We'd far rather neither have nor need them. But some of us clearly need to be in prison for the safety of the rest of us. As long as that's the case, we can, will and, indeed, must spend the money to do what it takes to incarcerate those people. Which means that breaking up with the tough law enforcement of the 1990s will be indeed be hard to do.

What Crimes Land Prisoners in Jail?

Over half of the increase in State prison populations since 1995 is due to an increase in prisoners convicted of violent offenses.

Violent offenses include murder, rape, sexual assault, robbery, assault, extortion, intimidation, criminal endangerment, and others.

Property offenses include burglary, larceny, motor vehicle theft, fraud, possession and selling of stolen property, destruction of property, trespassing, vandalism, criminal tampering, and others.

Drug offenses include possession, manufacturing, trafficking, and others.

Public-order offenses include weapons charges, drunk driving, escape/flight to avoid prosecution, court offenses, obstruction of justice charges, morals and decency charges, liquor law violations, and others.

Analyze the essay:

1. What statistics does Muhlhausen present to support his claim that prisons reduce crime?
2. How does the author tie his conclusion back to the introduction? What effect does this lend the essay?

Prisons Do Not Reduce Crime

Jim Holt

In the following essay Jim Holt maintains that modern U.S. prisons are barbaric and do little to deter crime. Holt challenges the notion that America's recent drop in crime is due to tough laws that imprison more offenders. Even states that did not pass strict prison-sentencing laws, he points out, experienced fewer crimes. Furthermore, he reasons, if harsh prison sentences deterred crime, then fewer newly released prisoners would commit new offenses—yet more released inmates have reoffended than before.

Holt writes for the *New Yorker*, the *New York Times Magazine*, and *Slate*, among other publications.

Consider the following questions:

1. According to the author, how were convicts punished in early England?
2. How much of the world's prison population does America account for, in Holt's opinion?
3. How does Holt describe the conditions in Finnish jails?

In the early 19th century, Europeans traveled to [U.S.] shores to marvel at a new institution called the "penitentiary," where inmates were to be reformed by a regime of silence and hard work. For a century and a half after the creation of prisons, crime dropped steadily across Western nations, even as the severity of punishment diminished. It seemed reasonable to think that as society grew

Jim Holt, "Decarcerate?" *New York Times Magazine*, August 15, 2004, pp. 20–21.

more prosperous and equitable, fewer and fewer people would have to be incarcerated.

But in the 1960's, for reasons scholars still debate, crime began to rise again. (This trend was not confined to the United States; it was also observed in most European countries.) And in response, our criminal justice system started getting more punitive. Legislators showed they were "tough on crime" by passing laws that mandated long sentences for even relatively minor offenses. In the late 70's, as more and more Americans were being crowded into lockup, states went on a prison-building spree. The inmate census doubled, then doubled again and again. Today, this nation keeps more than two million people behind bars—compared with only 200,000 three decades ago. With 5 percent of the world's population, we account for 25 percent of its prison population.

Due to overcrowded conditions in this Tracy, California, prison, officials have installed three-tiered bunks in a former recreation area in an effort to accommodate all the inmates.

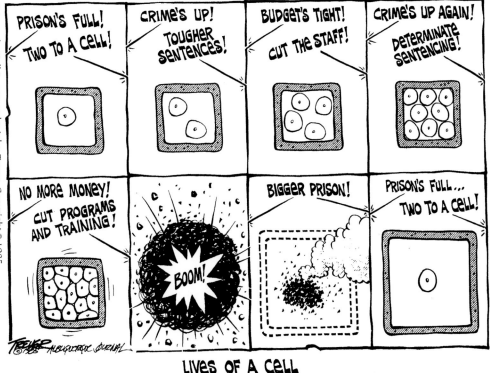

PRISON'S FULL! TWO TO A CELL!

CRIME'S UP! TOUGHER SENTENCES!

BUDGET'S TIGHT! CUT THE STAFF!

CRIME'S UP AGAIN! DETERMINATE SENTENCING!

NO MORE MONEY! CUT PROGRAMS AND TRAINING!

BOOM!

BIGGER PRISON!

PRISON'S FULL... TWO TO A CELL!

LIVES OF A CELL

Opposition to Prisons

There are some highly placed people who feel that the urge to incarcerate has gotten out of hand. Recently Supreme Court Justice Anthony M. Kennedy warned of "moral blindness" in the criminal justice system, and the American Bar Association has just issued a report calling for an end to mandatory minimum sentences and a renewed emphasis on rehabilitation (which recent studies have shown to be effective, despite the scoffing of many conservatives). But there seems to be little popular sentiment for scaling back our prison system too abruptly. After all, the great lockup has been accompanied by a falling crime rate [since 1994]. Troubled neighborhoods have become peaceful, and everyday life is more secure, at least from ordinary criminals.

Yet there is a movement afoot today, albeit a tiny one, that aspires to get rid of prisons altogether. The members

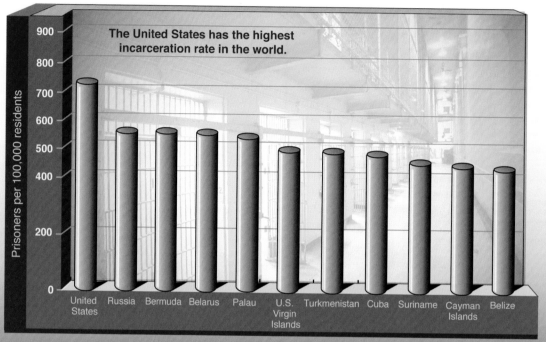

International Rates of Incarceration

The United States has the highest incarceration rate in the world.

Prisoners per 100,000 residents

| | United States | Russia | Bermuda | Belarus | Palau | U.S. Virgin Islands | Turkmenistan | Cuba | Suriname | Cayman Islands | Belize |

Source: International Centre for Prison Studies, 2005.

of this movement call themselves "abolitionists," borrowing the term applied to steadfast opponents of slavery before the Civil War. Since the 80's, an international group of abolitionists—lawyers, judges, criminologists—has been holding conferences every few years. According to "Instead of Prisons," published by the Prison Research Education Action Project in 1976, the first article of the abolitionist catechism is that imprisonment is morally objectionable and indefensible and must therefore be abolished. Are these people moral visionaries, like their 19th-century namesakes? Or are they simply nuts?

What's Wrong with Imprisonment

When you take a close look at the supposed justifications for punishment by imprisonment, you find that they don't hold up terribly well in theory or practice. Was the expansion of the prison population really responsible for the drop in crime [since 1994]? Then why did states that neglected to adopt tougher sentencing rules enjoy the same improvement as those that did? Do harsher sentences deter people from committing crimes? Then why did the recidivism rate—that is, the rate at which released prisoners commit new crimes—actually go up during the prison-building boom?

Even if the deterrent effect of imprisonment is overrated, there are those who feel that lawbreakers should nevertheless get stiff sentences because they deserve it. The idea of making an offender suffer for his crime can be traced to the "blood vengeance" practices of primitive societies. Today, it goes under the more dignified name of retribution, which literally means "paying back." How the suffering inflicted on an offender compensates for his crime has never been clear, unless it is through the vindictive satisfaction it might bring to his victims and society. But is this justice? There is increasing evidence that the most violent criminals are often driven by forces beyond their control. Because of damage to the frontal lobes of their brains caused by birth complications, accidents or brutal childhood beatings, they simply can't contain their aggressive impulses; compared with the rest of us, they live life on a neurological hair trigger. Clearly, society needs to protect itself from these people. But does it need to punish them?

Some abolitionists will concede that the prison system is a necessary evil for now. Their immediate goal is to decarcerate as many categories of prisoner as possible (nonviolent drug offenders, for instance), and to make prisons less debilitating and degrading for those who remain. But can we imagine the practice of coercive confinement withering away entirely? Will it ever

Prisons Are Not Necessarily Deterrents

There is no solid evidence to support the conclusion that sending more convicted offenders to prison for longer periods of time deters others from committing crime.

American Bar Association Task Force on Crime, quoted in Al Cunningham, "Black Imprisonment," Canadian Coalition Against the Death Penalty, April 29, 2001. www.ccadp.org.

The stark interior of a Finnish prison is pictured here. During the past thirty years, prison officials in Finland have become increasingly lenient in their treatment of inmates.

follow barbarous punishment like maiming, flogging and hanging into extinction?

Learning from Finland

If the very idea seems hopelessly utopian, consider a real-world case: Finland. Three decades ago, the Finns had a severe penal system modeled on that of the neighboring Soviet Union, and one of the highest imprisonment rates in Europe. Then they decided to rethink penal policy along more humane lines. Finnish prisons became almost ridiculously lenient by our standards. Inmates—referred to as "clients" or "pupils," depending on their age—live in dormitory-style rooms, address guards by the first name and get generous home leaves. "We believe that the loss of freedom is the major punishment, so we try to make it as nice inside as possible," one prison supervisor commented. Today, Finland imprisons the smallest fraction of its population of any European country (52 prisoners per 100,000 people, compared with 702 in the United States). Yet its crime rate, far from exploding, has remained at a low level.

That's a pretty impressive experiment in moral progress. As Winston Churchill observed, "Treatment of crime and criminals is one of the most unfailing tests of the civilization of any country." The American mode of treatment is starting to look less like a necessary evil and more like a peculiar institution.

Analyze the essay:

1. Identify the colorful language and descriptive details that make this article engaging. How do they affect the essay's overall persuasiveness?
2. Holt compares the idea of retribution to "the 'blood vengeance' practices of primitive societies." What point is he making with this comparison? Is it effective?
3. The author notes that Finland's nonpunitive legal system has kept that country's crime rate down. Why might it be difficult to compare different prison systems in different countries?

Prisons Should Rehabilitate Inmates

Ralph A. Rossum and Constance Rossum

Ralph A. Rossum and Constance Rossum are professors and members of the Statewide Inmate Family Council in California. In the essay that follows, they argue that prisons must focus on rehabilitation if released offenders are to become law-abiding citizens. The authors contend that prisons neglect to provide inmates with proper education or job training. Moreover, they claim, the lack of respect, empathy, and civility in prisons makes it difficult for inmates to improve themselves and learn to treat others respectfully. The likelihood of recidivism (criminals committing another offense) could be reduced, the Rossums suggest, if the purpose of prisons was to rehabilitate inmates.

Consider the following questions:

1. What were the results of the 2000 Gallup poll, according to the authors?
2. What facts do the Rossums provide to support their claim that prisoners are in desperate need of education?
3. Why are many vocational education programs unhelpful, in the authors' opinion?

Americans understand that the vast majority of inmates will one day be released from prison and, if they leave with better character, more education or vocational training, and better job skills than when they entered, that they will be more likely to avoid returning to crime, become independent and productive citizens, and contribute to the public good.

Why Are Prisons Failing?

Opinion polls make it clear that the public believes that prisons are failing badly in this respect. In a September 2000 Gallup Poll, 48 percent of respondents believed that prisons were doing a poor job "rehabilitating inmates so

This inmate has been imprisoned, released, and imprisoned again after committing further crimes. Critics point to cases such as his to argue that prisons fail to rehabilitate criminals.

they are less likely to commit crimes in the future." Another 34 percent said they were doing a fair job in this respect, with only 15 percent rating them as excellent or good. The public's perceptions match reality. A 2002 study by the Department of Justice's Bureau of Justice Statistics (BJS) reveals that 67 percent of all state prisoners released in 1994 had been rearrested, with 46.9 percent reconvicted, within three years.

Why Prisons Fail to Rehabilitate

There are two principal reasons why prisons are failing to rehabilitate inmates. The first and foremost is that rehabilitation seeks to improve the character of offenders, and the way most prisons treat prisoners degrades rather than improves their character. In his 1991 book, *On Character*, James Q. Wilson has defined character as empathy and self-control. Empathy refers to the ability to take into account the rights, needs, and feelings of others. Self-control refers to the ability to consider the more distant consequences of present actions—to be, in short, future-oriented rather than present-oriented. Most prisons do little to foster empathy and self-control; on the contrary, many of the actions taken by these huge, lumbering, and self-protecting bureaucracies undermine positive character formation.

> ## Prisons That are Focused on Punishment Fuel Violence
>
> The concern that we are attempting to resolve the issues of violence in America at the expense of creating violence and tension in our prisons is real. . . . Prisons . . . may turn nonviolent offenders into violent offenders.
>
> Kenneth L. McGinnis, *Building Violence: How America's Rush to Incarcerate Creates More Violence*, ed. John P. May. Thousand Oaks, CA: Sage, 2000.

Prisons Degrade Inmates

Take empathy, for example. While many guards display genuine humanity toward those they monitor, others do not. Some intentionally provoke fights among inmates, thereby triggering lockdowns, higher (hazardous duty) pay, and more overtime for themselves and fellow union members. Some engage in verbal harassment, discrimi-

nation, and retaliation. Others allow inmates to be brutalized by homosexual rape.

Thanks to court decisions based on equal protection and employment discrimination analyses, male officers are now assigned to female housing units and female officers to male housing units. As a consequence, some male guards use mandatory pat-frisks or room searches to grope female inmates' breasts, buttocks, and vaginal areas and to view them inappropriately while in a state of undress in the housing and bathroom areas and while showering, using the toilet, and changing sanitary napkins. The guards who undertake these and other violations of personal integrity do so with impunity; they know that corrections officers' unions are among the most powerful and politically connected special interest groups in the country and that their union will shield them from administrative sanctions.

A prison guard and inmate have a friendly talk. Though most guards treat prisoners professionally, there have been reports of some guards abusing inmates.

"No Pampering Prisoners," cartoon by Kirk Anderson. Copyright © 1995. Reproduced by permission.

How can inmates learn to empathize with the rights, needs, and feelings of others and not view their fellow citizens as mere objects to be exploited or harmed when so many of the guards regard them as objects of gratification, derision, and contempt? How can inmates learn to treat others with respect and civility in a prison culture that denigrates both?

Education Behind Bars

Prisons are also failing to foster a sense of self-control and future orientation in inmates. Few endeavors are as future-oriented as getting an education; it involves a disciplined effort that results in future rewards. It is not surprising that as prison sentences have become longer and in many cases have exceeded the time horizon of most inmates, the percentage of inmates participating in education programs has decreased.

Teaching prisoners skills that can be used in the outside world can be a first step toward rehabilitation. Here, two Illinois inmates learn how to weld, which could help them land jobs after they are released.

As a group, prison inmates are desperately in need of education; a 2003 BJS study reveals that 68 percent of state prison inmates do not have a high school diploma (compared with 18.4 percent of the general population). Yet, while the percentage of state prisons offering some form of educational programs increased from 88 in 1995 to 91.2 in 2002, the percentage of inmates participating in these programs actually declined from 56.6 in 1991 to 51.9 in 1997 in state prisons, and from 67 in 1991 to 56.4 in 1997 in federal prisons. The numbers are down across the board: for basic education, GED/high school courses, and especially for college courses. . . .

[This may be because] inmates face bureaucratic hurdles that may exhaust or trip them up. Inmates report that they are placed randomly into vocational educational programs because a slot is available, not because they have an interest or aptitude and often despite the fact that many of these programs are obsolete, preparing them for jobs that, as a result of modern technology, no longer exist. Others report that it can take up to a year to schedule a first meeting with a prison educational specialist to learn more about programs for which they are eligible. . . .

Rehabilitation Requires a Culture of Civility

We close with the second reason that prisons are failing to rehabilitate: the problem of the self-fulfilling prophecy. Research findings into the effectiveness of rehabilitation from the 1970s concluding that "nothing works" have taken deep root and have exonerated prison officials from even making the effort. Most prison systems have even eliminated altogether any reference to rehabilitation in their mission statements.

Having abandoned the rehabilitative ideal for long determinate sentences, prison officials have not only thrown away the key but also thrown in the towel on inmates. They seem unaware of the more recent scholarly literature that has challenged the "nothing works" conclusions of 30 years ago. This literature makes modest but critically important points. Claiming that rehabilitative programs can have a positive impact depending on the risk, need, and responsiveness of the treated inmates, it notes that appropriate correctional treatments yield lower levels of post-treatment recidivism than criminal penalties that involve no rehabilitative services.

Were prison officials to read this literature and take its conclusions to heart, they would realize that rehabilitation can be the result of incarceration even if it is not the reason. They would seek to establish within prisons a culture of respect and civility, for they would know that incarceration itself is the punishment, not what they do to the inmates who are under their control.

Analyze the essay:

1. Why do the Rossums present specific examples of indecencies that occur in prisons? How does this information impact their argument that prisons do not facilitate rehabilitation?
2. The authors argue that prisons are failing to rehabilitate criminals for what two reasons? Assess the evidence they present as support for these two reasons.

Prisons Should Punish Inmates

Charles Murray

Society has a duty to punish, not rehabilitate, criminals, claims Charles Murray in the following essay. He observes that in our current justice system, judges consider various factors when sentencing criminals, including whether they are remorseful and whether they will respond better to prison or to some alternative punishment. In Murray's view, convicts deserve to be jailed for committing certain offenses even if they will not or cannot commit more crimes.

Murray is the W.H. Brady Scholar at American Enterprise Institute, a think tank that advocates for individual liberty and responsibility as well as limited government.

Consider the following questions:

1. What does Una Padel say she wants from her daughter's muggers?
2. In Murray's opinion, why do communities exact retribution for crimes?
3. What are the core tenets of retributive justice, as Murray puts it?

I recently interviewed Una Padel, director of the Centre for Crime and Justice Studies, a research foundation that advocates alternatives to prison and restorative justice. A fortnight before we talked, her 13-year-old daughter had been mugged.

If the muggers could be brought to account (they cannot, even though the daughter knows who they are), what would Padel have in mind for them? True to her principles, she does not want the muggers jailed.

"I remain angry with them, but I don't want anything horrible to happen to them," she said. "I want them to stop robbing people that's the bottom line . . . In an ideal world I would like them to be made aware of the impact they've actually had on my daughter and, ideally, apologise."

Padel is no dewy-eyed naif. She has dealt with criminals for years and is easily as knowledgable and unsentimental as any judge likely to try the case. It's her own daughter who has suffered the harm.

Justice Is Not Therapy—It Is Punishment

I want to suggest a thought experiment: if she had the power, would Padel be morally entitled to give the muggers a sentence that does not punish them instead of one

This prisoner has committed multiple robberies and shown little remorse for his crimes. Many experts contend that such crimes deserve harsh, extended imprisonment.

that does? I am even willing to stipulate that her sentence inspires genuine remorse in the muggers and that they stop mugging (generous stipulations indeed). Would justice be done if Padel had her way?

The principles of the kind of simple justice I propose today say no. Justice does not consist of successful therapy. It consists of just deserts. The just desert for terrorising a 13-year-old and robbing her must entail punishment, whether or not the muggers feel bad about what they've done and whether or not they will do it again. . . .

Problems with Progressive Justice

[In our current system of progressive justice,] the judge is supposed to be able to . . . accurately assess whether the offender is really, truly sorry for what he did and is going to change his ways. It is an absurd premise. Indeed, even when the offender does feel genuine remorse, that doesn't mean the offender will stop offending. Two other characteristics of criminals are impulsiveness and a short time horizon. Offenders can be really, truly sorry for what they did today and be back on the streets doing it again a week from now. As police and probation officers will tell you, it happens all the time.

The judge is supposed to decide whether the offender will respond better to a community sentence or to prison. How? individual case histories of offenders reveal every kind of response, from the offender who is set straight by a tough prison sentence to the one who sees the error of his ways by apologising to his victim. A judge has to guess. I know judges prefer to call it the use of judicial discretion, not guessing—but guessing is what it really amounts to. Making matters worse, the guess usually reflects not the unique characteristics of the defendant and the offence, but the judge's personal ideology.

Everything I have said about judges applies equally to the people in the Crown Prosecution Service who are making decisions about whether to plea-bargain, drop charges or bring a case to trial.

For practical purposes, the question of whether the justice system should take personalities, background, remorse or predictions about future behaviour into account when deciding what should be done to an offender is moot. Whether or not it should, it can't. Prosecutors and judges cannot be that smart about the parade of offenders who come before them. Progressive justice doesn't do what it claims to do.

A judge doles out a sentence to a convicted criminal. Sentences can vary widely depending on a judge's ideas about appropriate punishment.

Retribution Through Punishment

The technical label for the simple alternative to progressive justice is "retributive justice". It is the modern version of the systems of justice that came into being at the dawn of human history, and it is based on the same reasoning.

The primal function of a system of justice is to depersonalise revenge. The agreement, perhaps the most ancient of all agreements that make it possible for communities to exist, is that the individual will take his complaint to the community. In return, the community will exact the appropriate retribution—partly on behalf of the wronged individual, but also to express the community's moral values. Justice means retribution—through punishment and upholding the supremacy of the good members of the community over the bad.

The word "retribution" is jarring to modern sensibility. Someone who wants retribution is harking back to the bad old days of an eye for an eye, we think. Retribution is something civilised societies ought to rise above. The victim's desire for retribution is atavistic [reverting to the past] and unworthy.

Is it? As a way of testing your own views, consider a thought experiment that Immanuel Kant, the German philosopher, posed two centuries ago. He imagined an island society that is to disband tomorrow. Its citizens must decide whether a murderer awaiting execution should be executed. (If you're against the death penalty, substitute some other suitable punishment.) Executing him will have no expedient benefit for members of the society. It will certainly have no benefit for the prisoner.

We will assume that the prisoner, if released, will not kill again. The only purpose of the punishment is retribution. Should the murderer be executed? Kant says yes, that "the last murderer remaining in prison must first be executed so that everyone will duly receive what his actions are worth". What do you say?

Criminals Deserve Punishment

This way of looking at the function of justice has a distinguished intellectual pedigree, but the principle itself is deeply ingrained in most people's sense of the rightness of things. It feels instinctively wrong when someone does something bad and gets away with it. When we say that someone "gets away with it", we mean that the person suffers no punishment or too little punishment.

The core tenets of retributive justice are simple. The necessary and sufficient justification for punishing criminals is that they did something for which they deserve punishment. Here "something" refers to the behaviours that society has defined as offences; "deserve" means that the offenders are culpable—morally responsible.

Most people believe in retributive justice, feeling strongly that criminals like this teen must be punished for their crimes.

Society not only has the right to punish culpable offenders; the moral responsibility of the offender imposes on society the duty to punish.

That's it. Nothing about rehabilitation, remorse or socioeconomic disadvantage.

Nothing about the bad effects that the punishment might have on the offender or, for that matter, its good effects. The purpose of a sentence is punishment. When a system fails to punish culpable offenders, it has failed, full stop. It is unjust.

Analyze the essay:

1. The author begins his piece with the real-life story of Una Padel and her thirteen-year-old daughter who was mugged. What purpose does this example serve?
2. How does the author use rhetorical questions and scenarios to encourage readers to think about justice? Is this technique effective?
3. Consider Immanuel Kant's example as set forth by Murray. Would you punish the last remaining murderer on a deserted island? Why?

Three-Strikes Laws Have Led to Excessive Imprisonment

Vincent Schiraldi and Geri Silva

Three-strikes laws mandate a twenty-five-years-to-life imprisonment of certain offenders for their third felony conviction. According to Vincent Schiraldi and Geri Silva in the following article, this law has been applied to far too many nonviolent offenders, such as burglars and drug addicts. Moreover, Schiraldi and Silva contend, three-strikes laws do not effectively reduce crime. They also claim that the law is unfairly applied, impacting minorities more than whites. The financial and social costs of locking up non-violent offenders, they reason, are too great to justify.

Schiraldi is executive director of the Justice Policy Institute, and Silva is executive director of Families to Amend California's Three Strikes.

Consider the following questions:

1. What have been the effects of three-strikes laws, according to the Justice Policy Institute's report?
2. In the authors' opinion, how much more likely are African Americans to be sentenced to life imprisonment under three-strikes laws than whites?
3. What is the financial cost of incarcerating offenders under California's three-strikes laws, as cited by the authors?

Three weeks after California's three-strikes law was enacted in March 1994, Brian Smith was charged with abetting a petty theft after his two companions were

Vincent Schiraldi and Geri Silva, "Three Strikes: Law That Fails on All Counts," *Los Angeles Times*, March 7, 2004, p. M2. Reproduced by permission of the authors.

caught shoplifting in a convenience store. The offense usually carries a short jail term. But it landed Smith in prison for 25 years to life.

That's because the new law counted the petty-theft crime as Smith's third felony conviction. When 19, he had committed a strong-arm robbery (no weapon or physical harm involved). Five years later, he was convicted of burglarizing an unoccupied dwelling. These two offenses plus the petty theft sent Smith to prison until at least 2014. If Smith stays healthy, and he is released after serving his absolute minimum time (far from likely in California), his imprisonment for petty theft will have cost the state more than $600,000.

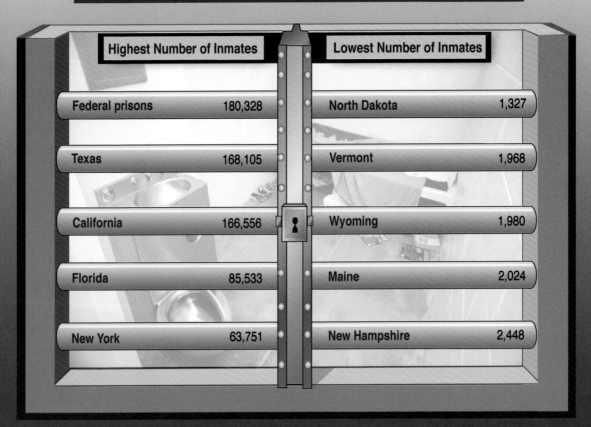

A Comparison of Prison Populations in America

Highest Number of Inmates		Lowest Number of Inmates	
Federal prisons	180,328	North Dakota	1,327
Texas	168,105	Vermont	1,968
California	166,556	Wyoming	1,980
Florida	85,533	Maine	2,024
New York	63,751	New Hampshire	2,448

Source: Bureau of Justice Statistics, "Prisoners in 2004," October 2005.

An Ineffective Law

Three strikes turns 10 today [March 7, 2004], and in light of research on its budgetary and law enforcement effects, as well as the experiences of legions of Brian Smiths, it has had a troubled childhood. According to a report released last week by the Justice Policy Institute, three strikes has contributed heavily to California's chronic prison population growth, has been applied disproportionately to African Americans and Latinos and has had little effect on crime rates. Ironically, although the law purported to go after California's most violent criminals, nonviolent offenders sentenced under the law outnumber violent ones by nearly 2 to 1.

With the state facing a budget gap of $7 billion to $8 billion [in 2004], and with little evidence that the three-strikes law is living up to its billing as an efficient crime fighter, California should consider amending it.

Examining Crime Rates

The crime rate has declined in California since 1994, but it would be a big stretch to credit three strikes. Among California's 12 largest counties, the six most frequent users of the law "struck out" defendants at twice the rate of the lowest. If three strikes was truly a factor in curbing violent crime, these heavy-using counties should have experienced a sharper drop in such crime than the light users. The opposite happened. In counties that sparingly used three strikes, the decline in violent crime was 23% greater than in heavy-using ones. For example, defendants "struck out" in L.A. County at nine times the rate in San Francisco, yet the violent-crime rate dropped 24% more in San Francisco County from 1993 to 2002.

That pattern held when comparing states that have three-strikes laws with those that don't. Between 1993 and 2002, the latter experienced a decline in violent crime that was 30% higher than the former. The decline in violent crime in New York, which doesn't have a three-strikes law, was 20% greater than in California. Even after eight years, states without a three-strikes measure had an average violent crime rate 30% below California's.

Unjust Imprisonment

One possible reason for three strikes' disappointing performance as a crime fighter is that 65% of those incarcerated under the law during its first decade committed nonviolent crimes. There are more Californians serving a life sentence under the law for drug possession than for second-degree murder, assault with a deadly weapon and rape combined. Some 354 inmates are serving life for Smith's conviction—petty theft of under $250.

Donnell Dorsey's case, reported in *The Times*, illustrates how suddenly and dramatically the penalties changed for nonviolent offenders after three strikes was enacted. On March 7, 1994, hours after three strikes became law, Dorsey faced a life sentence after being arrested for receiving stolen property. If nabbed earlier in the day, he would have faced a maximum term of six years, with the chance of only three years if he behaved while in prison.

Duane Silva, who is borderline mentally retarded, stole a neighbor's VCR and some antique coins days after three strikes became law. Leandro Andrade shoplifted nine videotapes in 1995. In 1997, Shane Reams aided in the sale of $20 worth of crack cocaine to an undercover officer. All are serving life sentences.

Three strikes' draconian approach has landed more heavily on people of color. African Americans are sentenced to life under three strikes at 12 times the rate of whites, a disparity far greater than any found in other criminal justice policies. Latinos are 78% more likely to be sentenced under three strikes than whites. In many ways, the incremental racial dispar-

---

Three-Strikes Laws Violate Prisoner Rights

If there's a prisoner rights issue that screams for redress it's three strikes. . . . The draconian law blatantly violates the 8th Amendment prohibition against cruel and unusual punishment.

Earl Ofari Hutchinson, "Supreme Court Should Strike Out Three Strikes," AlterNet, November 11, 2002. www.alternet.org.

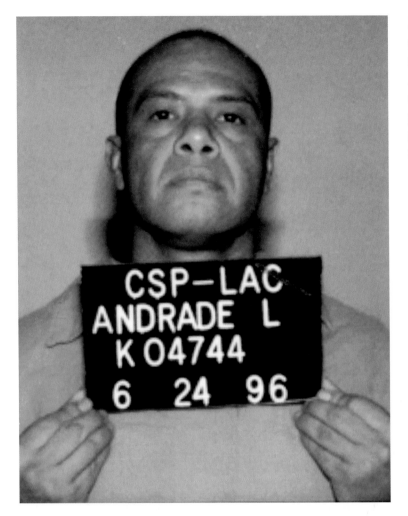

Because of California's three-strikes law, repeat offender Leandro Andrade received a fifty-year prison sentence for stealing nine video-tapes.

ities evident in the overall criminal-justice process combine geometrically in three strikes enforcement, resulting in such gross disproportionality of application.

The High Cost of Three-Strikes Laws

All this comes at an enormous cost to Californians. Currently, more than one in four inmates were sentenced under three strikes. The cost of their incarceration will be $8 billion more than it would be if three strikes were not on the books. Nearly $5 billion of that will be spent strik-ing out nonviolent offenders.

A girl protests the lengthy prison sentence her father received for possessing a small amount of drugs. One complaint about three-strikes laws is that they extend the time parents are away from their children.

Finally, three strikes exacts a heavy toll on prisoners' families. Some 46,700 children will spend an additional 5.8 years away from their parents as a result of the law. According to the California Research Bureau, children of incarcerated parents can suffer "emotional withdrawal, failure in school, delinquency and risk of intergenerational incarceration."

Three strikes has proved to be overly broad, costly and ineffective. The law should apply only to those convicted of violent offenses. That would free money for schools and healthcare.

Analyze the essay:

1. Schiraldi and Silva profile specific people who have been sentenced under three-strikes laws. What do these real-life examples add to their argument? Which examples did you find most striking, and why?

2. What facts do the authors provide to support their assertion that three-strikes laws do not reduce crime?

Three-Strikes Laws Have Not Led to Excessive Imprisonment

Chuck Poochigian

Three-strikes laws can put offenders behind bars for 25 years to life for their third felony. In the following selection Chuck Poochigian, a Republican California senator, refutes the notion that these laws imprison too many offenders. He explains that such laws have jailed only criminals who have committed at least two serious or violent felonies—people who should be imprisoned, in his view. The incarceration of habitual criminals, he insists, demonstrates that there are consequences for breaking the law and protects citizens from becoming victims of crime. As a result of three-strikes measures, crime rates are at their lowest level in thirty-five years, maintains Poochigian, and taxpayers have been spared billions of dollars in the cost of crime.

Consider the following questions:

1. What serious or violent felonies does the author say count as first or second strikes?
2. How does Poochigian respond to protests that third strikes are triggered by felonies that are not serious or violent?
3. According to the author, who would be eligible for resentencing and possible release if California's three-strikes law were amended by Proposition 66?

California's crime rates are at historic lows, having improved dramatically over the last 10 years since the state's voters overwhelmingly approved the "Three

Chuck Poochigian, "No: Law Is a Big Help in the Deterrence of Repeat Cases," *Fresno Bee*, July 28, 2004, p. B9. Copyright © The McClatchy Company 2004. Reproduced by permission.

Strikes and You're Out" law. This groundbreaking measure established a sensible but tough new approach to dealing with habitual lawbreakers that has locked thousands of felons behind bars for 25 years to life.

Unfortunately, it took the tragic slaying of a young girl in 1992 by a dangerous repeat offender to draw public attention to the problem and galvanize support behind a measure to keep chronic criminals off our streets and in jail. In November 1994, the initiative establishing the

Richard Allen Davis (pictured) kidnapped and murdered twelve-year-old Polly Klaas in 1993, which led to the passing of California's three-strikes law.

"Three Strikes" law passed by a landslide with more than 76% of the vote.

The concept behind "Three Strikes" is simple: Habitual criminals should receive more severe penalties. Criminals receive a first or second strike when they commit serious or violent felonies such as murder, rape, lewd acts on a child, assault with a deadly weapon on a peace officer, sale to a minor of drugs like cocaine and PCP, and carjacking.

Conviction of a second strike offense results in a sentence enhancement, effectively doubling the penalty. A third strike is earned for any felony if the criminal has been convicted of at least two previous serious or violent felonies and can result in a sentence of 25 years to life.

Since the implementation of "three strikes," the overall crime rate per 100,000 residents in California has been reduced to its lowest levels in 35 years. Most major crimes have decreased by 50% or more.

Undermine the Law

Despite the demonstrated success of this tough-on-crime measure, an effort is underway to significantly weaken California's "Three Strikes" law. Proposition 66, which will appear on the November 2004 ballot, would undermine key components of the law.[1]

The initiative's proponents have focused on the requirement that the felony for which third-strike penalties are triggered must not always be serious or violent. However, judges and prosecutors already have substantial discretion to avert application of "Three Strikes" in the furtherance of justice if the facts surrounding a third felony conviction clearly do not warrant such a sentence.

Opponents of "Three Strikes" also argue that this system has led to excessive incarceration rates. This assertion is simply not supported by the facts. A March 2004 report by the Department of Corrections identifies only 7,372 inmates incarcerated in state prison for a third

1. Proposition 66 was defeated by 53 percent of voters.

strike conviction, representing 4.5% of the total inmate prison population. At the same time, 32,158 persons convicted of second strikes were incarcerated, more than four times the number of third-strikers.

Given today's awful 70%-plus recidivism rate in California (the highest in the United States), the fact that less than 25% of second strikers return to prison with a third strike is evidence that this policy is working.

One of the most disturbing effects of the proposed weakening of California's "Three Strikes" law is that it would retroactively reduce six crimes from "serious and violent" felonies to straight felonies that would not invoke application of "Three Strikes."

This means that approximately 25,000 convicted second- and third-strike felons will be eligible for resentencing and potential release into our cities and streets. These criminals have been convicted of such crimes as felony arson, residential burglary, criminal threats, gang-related crimes and some felonies in which great bodily injury occurs.

California Governor Arnold Schwarzenegger is an ardent supporter of California's three-strikes law. Here, he campaigns against a measure that sought to repeal the law.

Supporters of three-strikes laws say they keep repeat criminals like serial murderer Daniel Troyer (left) off the streets.

A Different Story

California's "Three Strikes" law has proven to be a strong deterrent to repeat offenders, raising intense awareness among previously convicted felons about the consequences they may suffer if convicted of a third felony.

We should continue to explore ways to improve our criminal justice system and to ensure that criminals who are going to be returning to our streets have been given the skills needed to avoid a life of crime. But there should be no mistake about the fact that repeat offenders with a history of serious and violent crime convictions represent a different story. It is likely that criminals who are lifetime offenders will continue to prey on society and wreak havoc with the lives of innocent victims and their families, unless subjected to long-term confinement.

A primary responsibility of state government is to protect the lives and safety of its citizens. Opponents of "Three Strikes" typically use the added cost of housing felons as a key factor in their arsenal of excuses to do away with the law. This argument is debunked by cost-of-crime figures from the U.S. Department of Justice, which suggest that "Three Strikes" has saved California taxpayers billions of dollars.

In any case, the assessment of the cost of incarceration must be weighed against the pain, anguish and expense borne by victims of the perpetrators of crime.

Any attempt to alter this life-saving, tough-on-crime measure should not be taken lightly. Tinkering with this monumental crime control measure in the way that Proposition 66 suggests would have serious, adverse consequences, and could potentially release many thousands of dangerous felons into our state.

The "Three Strikes and You're Out" law has successfully ended the revolving door of California's criminal justice system and has been instrumental in keeping the most violent repeat felons off of our streets. The law works, and for the safety or our citizens it should be preserved.

Analyze the essay:

1. What cause-and-effect relationships can you find in this article? What phrases does Poochigian use to signify cause-and-effect relationships?

2. When discussing three-strikes laws, this author focuses on the pain and anguish of victims of crime to support his view that three-strikes laws should be upheld. On the other hand, Schiraldi and Silva in the previous article mention the toll that incarceration takes on offenders and their families to back up their argument that the laws should be repealed. With which viewpoint do you most identify? Why?

Section Two:
Model Essays
and Writing
Exercises

The Five-Paragraph Essay

An essay is a short piece of writing that discusses or analyzes one topic. The five-paragraph essay is a form commonly used in school assignments and tests. Every five-paragraph essay begins with an introduction, ends with a conclusion, and features three supporting paragraphs in the middle.

The Thesis Statement. The introduction includes the essay's thesis statement. The thesis statement presents the argument or point the author is trying to make about the topic. The essays in this book all have different thesis statements because they are making different arguments about prisons.

The thesis statement should clearly tell the reader what the essay will be about. A focused thesis statement helps determine what will be in the essay; the subsequent paragraphs are spent developing and supporting its argument.

The Introduction. In addition to presenting the thesis statement, a well-written introductory paragraph captures the attention of the reader and explains why the topic being explored is important. It may provide the reader with background information on the subject matter or feature an anecdote that illustrates a point relevant to the topic. It could also present startling information that clarifies the point of the essay or puts forth a contradictory position that the essay will refute. Further techniques for writing an introduction are found later in this section.

The Supporting Paragraphs. The introduction is then followed by three (or more) supporting paragraphs. These comprise the main body of the essay. Each paragraph presents and develops a subtopic that supports the essay's thesis statement. Each subtopic is then supported with its own facts, details, and examples. The writer can use various kinds of supporting material and details to back up the topic of each supporting paragraph. These may include statistics, quotations from people with special knowledge or expertise, historic facts, and anecdotes. A rule of writing is that specific and concrete examples are more convincing than vague, general, or unsupported assertions.

The Conclusion. The conclusion is the paragraph that closes the essay. Its function is to summarize or reiterate the main idea of the essay. It may recall an idea from the introduction or briefly examine the larger implications of the thesis. Because the conclusion is also the last chance a writer has to make an impression on the reader, it is important that it not simply repeat what has been presented elsewhere in the essay but close it in a clear, final, and memorable way.

Although the order of the essay's component paragraphs is important, they do not have to be written in that order. Some writers like to decide on a thesis and write the introduction paragraph first. Other writers like to focus first on the body of the essay and write the introduction and conclusion later.

Pitfalls to Avoid

When writing essays about controversial issues such as prisons, it is important to remember that disputes over the material are common precisely because there are many different perspectives. Remember to state your arguments in careful and measured terms. Evaluate your topic fairly—avoid overstating negative qualities of one perspective or understating positive qualities of another. Use examples, facts, and details to support any assertions you make.

The Cause-and-Effect Essay

The previous section of this book provided you with samples of published persuasive writing on prisons. All were persuasive, or opinion, essays advocating certain positions on prisons. They were also either cause-and-effect essays or used cause-and-effect reasoning. This section will focus on writing your own cause-and-effect essay.

Cause and effect is a common method of organizing and explaining ideas and events. Simply put, cause and effect is a relationship between two things in which one thing makes something else happen. The cause is the reason something happens. The effect is what happens as a result.

A simple example would be a car not starting because it is out of gas. The lack of gas is the cause; the failure to start is the effect. Another example of cause-and-effect reasoning is found in Viewpoint One by David Muhlhausen. He argues that America's increased imprisonment of criminals since 1980 led to a subsequent drop in crime. Jailing more offenders is the cause; a reduction in crime is the effect.

Not all cause-and-effect relationships are as clear-cut as these two examples. It can be difficult to determine the cause of an effect, especially when talking about society-wide causes and effects. For example, smoking and cancer have been long associated with each other, but not all cancer patients smoke, and not all smokers get cancer. It took decades of debate and research before the U.S. surgeon general concluded in 1964 that smoking cigarettes causes cancer (and even then, that conclusion was disputed by tobacco companies for many years thereafter). Many other causes and effects are unclear and thus disputed. For example, in this book Jim Holt in Viewpoint Two challenges the notion that imprisoning more offenders leads to a decline in crime. He notes that crime is down overall, even in states that have not jailed more criminals. He also observes that an increased number of released inmates go on to commit more offenses once they leave prison. Therefore, Holt concludes, prisons are not responsible for a reduction in crime. Whether prisons deter crime is a matter of ongoing debate, and separating the causes from the effects can be a difficult task in any debate. Creating and evaluating cause-and-effect arguments involves both collecting evidence and exercising critical thinking.

Types of Cause-and-Effect Essays

Cause-and-effect essays are distinguished from other types of essays by how the thesis and its supporting arguments are organized. In general, there are three types of cause-and-effect essays. The thesis statement of the essay should make clear what kind of cause-and-effect essay is being written.

In one type, many causes can contribute to a single effect. Supporting paragraphs each examine one specific cause. For example, Ralph A. Rossum and Constance Rossum in Viewpoint Three mention several factors that, in their view, cause prisons to be ineffective in deterring criminals from committing additional offenses. In their opinion, prison authorities degrade inmates, fail to teach them how self-discipline results in future rewards, and do not make rehabilitation a goal of imprisonment. The effect of these multiple factors is that released inmates are often rearrested and reconvicted within three years, according to the Rossums. In their view, this raises doubt about the effectiveness of punitive prisons.

Another type of cause-and-effect essay examines multiple effects from a single cause. This is a good approach when discussing an event or circumstance that has several results. An example from this volume is found in Viewpoint Five. Vincent Schiraldi and Geri Silva maintain that the passage of three-strikes laws, which mandate prison time for certain offenders on their third felony conviction, has had several negative effects. For example, they provide statistics to show that the laws have caused far too many nonviolent offenders to be imprisoned who do not deserve to be, have led to the imprisonment of many more minorities than whites, and have burdened taxpayers with the increased costs of incarcerating these offenders.

A third type of cause-and-effect essay describes a series of causes and effects—a "chain of events" in which each link is both the effect of what happened before and the cause of what happens next. For instance, Chuck Poochigian in Viewpoint Six examines the consequences of amending California's three-strikes law. He claims that changing certain requirements of the law (the initial cause) would make about twenty-five thousand convicted felons eligible for resentencing (an effect). According to Poochigian, many of these criminals would then be released back into communities where they could continue to terrorize innocent victims (a subsequent effect). Based on this chain of events, he predicts that crime rates would rise (the ultimate effect) if the three-strikes law were revised.

Tips to Remember

When writing persuasive essays about controversial issues such as prisons, it is important to remember that disputes over cause-and-effect relationships are part of the controversy. Issues concerning prisons are complex and have multiple effects and multiple causes. Often people disagree over the causes. One needs to be careful and measured in how arguments are expressed. Avoid overstating cause-and-effect relationships if they are unwarranted.

Another pitfall to avoid when writing cause-and-effect essays is to mistake chronology for causation. Just because event X came before event Y does not necessarily mean that X caused Y. Additional evidence may be needed, such as documented studies or similar testimony from many people. Likewise, correlation does not necessarily imply causation. Just because two events happened at the same time does not necessarily mean they are causally related. Again, additional evidence is needed to verify the cause-and-effect argument.

In the following section you will read model essays on prisons that use cause-and-effect arguments and complete exercises that will help you write your own essay.

Words and Phrases Common in Cause-and-Effect Essays

Writers use these words to show the relationship between cause and effect, to provide transitions between paragraphs, and to summarize key ideas in an essay's concluding paragraph.

accordingly	it then follows that
as a result of	since
because	so
consequently	so that
due to	subsequently
for	therefore
for this reason	this is how
if . . . then	thus

Unjust Laws Cause Unnecessary Imprisonment

Editor's Notes A multiple-cause essay examines several factors that cause an event or result. Essay one is a multiple-cause essay structured in five paragraphs. In the essay, the author argues that three different types of laws—mandatory-minimum sentencing laws, three-strikes laws, and truth-in-sentencing laws—cause a large number of Americans to be incarcerated. However, many of these people do not belong in prisons, according to the author. Each paragraph includes supporting details and quotations, some of which were gathered from the viewpoints found in Section One.

Note that all sources are cited using Modern Language Association (MLA) style. For more information on how to cite your sources, see Appendix C.* As you read this essay, pay attention to its components. The sidebar notes are meant to help you better understand the essay's organization. Also consider the following questions:

1. What phrases used in the essay indicate a cause-and-effect relationship?
2. What kinds of evidence are provided to support the writer's argument?
3. Is the conclusion effective, in your opinion? Why?

■ Refers to thesis and topic sentences

■ Refers to supporting details

Paragraph 1

As a result of "get-tough-on-crime" legislation, more than 2 million people are now incarcerated in America's prisons. Nonviolent offenders make up the majority of the prison population. In fact, according to the Bureau of Justice, only 10 percent of federal prisoners in 2000 were serving time for a violent offense. Three unnecessarily harsh laws called mandatory-minimum sentencing laws, three-strikes laws,

The author establishes in the opening paragraph why this topic should matter to readers.

This is the essay's thesis statement.

* In applying MLA style, the following simplifications have been made: Parenthetical text citations are confined to direct quotations only; electronic source documentation in the Works Cited list omits page ranges and some detailed facts of publication.

and truth-in-sentencing laws are directly responsible for the mass incarceration of Americans who have not committed serious crimes. Confined in horrid, often overcrowded cells, these inmates are vulnerable to abuse from both prison guards and other prisoners. Because prisons are such violent places, they should be reserved for only the most hardened and dangerous criminals, not minor offenders who pose little threat to society.

Paragraph 2

The writer must explain the law before convincing readers of its unfairness.

Mandatory-minimum sentencing laws are the most stringent laws that subject nonviolent offenders to jail time. Enacted in the 1980s in an attempt to standardize sentences around the country, these laws mandate a set amount of prison time for specific crimes. They prevent judges from considering the particular circumstances of each case that might have otherwise resulted in more or less jail time.

A specific example of mandatory-minimum sentencing laws is provided.

A particularly alarming example of these laws is the case of New Yorker Justin D. Powell, who had pled guilty to two charges of possessing crack cocaine when he was a minor. Then, at thirty-two years old, he was caught dealing crack. Instead of sending him to a rehabilitation program where he could get the help he needed for his drug problem, Judge David Hurd was forced to issue him a sentence of life in prison. This punishment surely does not fit Powell's crime.

Citing an authority like the ABA lends credence to the author's argument.

Institutions such as the American Bar Association (ABA) have called for the repeal of mandatory minimums. The laws are also opposed by a whopping 86 percent of federal judges (Holt 20–21).

Paragraph 3

Referring back to the idea in the previous paragraph helps transition between paragraphs.

Much like mandatory-minimum legislation, three-strikes laws cause some offenders to serve unfair prison sentences. These laws apply to people convicted of their third felonies. In states such as California, three-strikes laws double the sentences for anyone who commits a third felony if one of their three offenses was serious or violent. They may also require a twenty-five-years-to-life sentence for offenders whose previous two felonies were serious or violent.

Note the adjectives the author uses to convey her opinion of three-strikes laws.

This can result in wildly inappropriate

sentences. Brian Smith, for example, was sentenced in 1994 to twenty-five years to life in prison for his third strike of abetting a petty theft in a convenience store. His first strike had been an unarmed robbery at age nineteen, his second offense was burglary of an unoccupied dwelling. Although few people would defend his actions, it is unfair that he will spend decades in prison while child abuser Vanessa Jackson, initially charged with twenty-eight counts of child endangerment and aggravated assault, will be eligible for parole after serving just two years. As three-strikes opponents Vincent Schiraldi and Geri Silva put it, "Three strikes has proved to be overly broad, costly and ineffective" (Schiraldi M2). Indeed, three strikes and you're out is one policy that has caused prison populations to unnecessarily explode.

Quotes should be worked into your essay as seamlessly as possible. Note how the author incorporates this quote from Viewpoint Five.

Paragraph 4

Yet another set of laws can be blamed for filling prisons to capacity: truth-in-sentencing laws, which aim to keep Americans imprisoned for longer periods of time. The laws require certain convicts to serve the majority of their sentence—usually 85 percent of it—before becoming eligible for probation or parole. But nonviolent offenders should at least be eligible for early release. Giving prisoners hope of early release motivates them to follow the rules and to take steps to better themselves while imprisoned. Furthermore, detaining nonviolent offenders behind bars unfairly burdens taxpayers, who must pay to keep them there. In Wisconsin alone, truth-in-sentencing laws racked up nearly $400 million in extra costs since 2000, according to Zahn and Barton. Clearly, truth-in-sentencing laws are both fiscally and morally irresponsible.

This is the topic sentence of the fourth paragraph.

The last sentence ties together the paragraph's arguments.

Paragraph 5

Mandatory-minimum, three-strikes, and truth-in-sentencing laws lead to the lengthy incarceration of many Americans who do not belong alongside vicious murderers and rapists. It is understandable that lawmakers wish to punish wrongdoers for their crimes. However, these

Note how the writer restates the thesis without exactly repeating it.

particular laws subject nonviolent offenders to the perils of prison and force judges to ignore mitigating circumstances. Our criminal justice system is supposed to be about judicial discretion, not about blindly feeding the already monstrous prison complex. Let's implement laws that reflect that sentiment.

Works Cited

Bureau of Justice. "Criminal Offenders Statistics." 13 Nov. 2005, accessed 11 Oct, 2006 < www.ojp.usdoj.gov/bjs/crimoff.htm > .

Holt, Jim. "Decarcerate?" New York Times Magazine 15 Aug. 2004: 20–21.

Schiraldi, Vincent, and Geri Silva. "Three Strikes: Law That Fails on All Counts." Los Angeles Times 7 Mar. 2004. M2.

Zahn, Mary, and Gina Barton. "Tougher Sentencing Law Carries Hefty Price." JSOnline. 20 Nov. 2004. < www.jsonline.com/story/index.asp?id=270059&format=print > .

Exercise A: Create an Outline from an Existing Essay

It often helps to create an outline of your essay before you write it. The outline can help you organize the information, arguments, and evidence you have gathered with your research.

For this exercise, create an outline that could have been used to write Essay One: "Unjust Laws Cause Unnecessary Imprisonment." This "reverse-engineering" exercise will help familiarize you with how outlines can be used to organize information.

To do this you will need to articulate the essay's thesis, identify important pieces of evidence, and take note of cause-and-effect relationships in the argument. Part of the outline has already been started to give you an idea of the assignment.

Outline

Write the essay's thesis:

I. Introduction:

II. Paragraph 2's main argument: Mandatory-minimum sentencing laws subject offenders to jail time unjustly.
   A.
      1. Example of Justin D. Powell
      2.
III. Paragraph 3's main argument:
   A. Results in inappropriate sentences
      1.
      2. Schiraldi and Silva's quote about the drawbacks of three-strikes laws
IV. Paragraph 4's main argument:
   A.
      1. Prisoners are better behaved and more motivated
      2.
V. Conclusion. Write the essay's conclusion:

Heavy Sentences Help America

Refers to thesis
and topic
sentences

Refers to
supporting
details

Editor's Notes Model Essay Two is an example of a multiple-effect essay. In it, the author claims that sentencing criminals to prison has three positive effects on society. Like the first model essay, Essay Two consists of five paragraphs with one introductory paragraph, one concluding paragraph, and three supporting paragraphs. Many of the facts presented here were collected from the viewpoints found in Section One.

The sidebar notes and questions will help you analyze how this essay is written and organized.

Paragraph 1

Why do you think the author chose to begin her essay with this anecdote?

In early 2006, Vermont judge Edward Cashman presided over a child molestation case that captured the country's attention. Although Mark Hulett had sexually abused a young girl regularly for four years, he received the shortest possible sentence allowed: Sixty days in prison, plus a treatment program for sex offenders. Following a national outcry, Cashman increased the sentence to a minimum of three years, less than the amount of time Hulett spent molesting his victim. With sentences like Hulett's being handed out, it is no wonder that so many criminals repeat their aberrant behavior. As British journalist Peter Hitchens points out, "Wrongdoers come to believe that . . . they can misbehave without any consequences" (Hitchens 62). In order to prevent crime and lawlessness we must not hesitate to sentence criminals to substantial amounts of jail time. Incarcerating criminals has three positive effects on society: It helps achieve retribution for their crimes, it incapacitates them, and it discourages other people from committing crimes.

What is the essay's thesis statement?

Paragraph 2

Sentencing criminals to jail time makes them appropriately pay for their crimes. Justice can be achieved for victims only when the criminals who caused their suffering are seriously punished. Jean Lewis, former president of Parents of Murdered Children, argues, "Society must have the courage to take a stand, denounce [crime] as abhorrent, vow not to tolerate it and follow through with a tough sentence." Jailing a wrongdoer not only serves the victim, but it allows communities to set standards for what is wrong and right. Explains Charles Murray of the American Enterprise Institute, it is the community's responsibility to "exact the appropriate retribution—partly on behalf of the wronged individual, but also to express the community's moral values. Justice means retribution through punishment and upholding the supremacy of the good members of the community over the bad" (Murray 1). A society unwilling to impose serious prison sentences on criminals is one in which injustice prevails.

From what authorities does the author quote?

Murray's quote from Viewpoint Four supports the paragraph's thesis. Be sure to retain information that you can quote to back up your arguments.

Paragraph 3

An equally important purpose of extended prison sentences is to protect the public from dangerous predators. After all, if a rapist or murderer is kept behind bars, he cannot terrorize the community. Senior policy analyst David Muhlhausen of the Heritage Foundation estimates that each imprisonment prevents approximately seventeen new crimes a year. He notes that when the prison population increases by 10 percent, the murder rate decreases by 13 percent. From these statistics, he concludes that "millions of people have avoided becoming victims of such crimes thanks to these policies [of imprisoning offenders]." Sequestering felons in facilities where they cannot injure the public is nothing less than a matter of common sense.

What is the topic sentence of Paragraph 3?

Note how the writer incorporates these statistics from Viewpoint One. What impact do they have on the paragraph's argument?

Paragraph 4

Not only do prisons shield citizens from violent criminals, they discourage other people from committing crimes too. When citizens realize that wrongdoers are punished with harsh prison terms, they are much less likely to break laws themselves. A youth who sees her neighbors sentenced

What transitions does the author use to keep the essay moving from one idea to another?

to twenty years for aiding an armed robbery or dealing crack cocaine, for example, will certainly think twice before engaging in crime. As Hitchens suggests, restoring the notion that prisons are for punishment "would prevent many young people from falling into the fumbling hands of the criminal justice system—because they would not risk getting into trouble in the first place" (Hitchens 62). Conversely, the opposite effect happens when criminal-minded members of the community see child molesters or murderers let off with light sentences—it sends a weak message about crime.

What is the topic sentence of Paragraph 4?

Paragraph 5

How does the author restate the essay's thesis without repeating it exactly from the introduction?

Why do you think the author chose to end the essay with questions? Is this method effective, in your opinion?

For all of these reasons, sentencing must include extended prison time. When judges unabashedly offer jail time as punishment, victims are at least partly recompensed for their grief, criminals are incapacitated, and additional crimes are prevented. Without tough prison sentences, child rapists such as Mark Hulett get a slap on the wrist and effectively get away with their transgressions. Do law-abiding American citizens really want men like Hulett walking freely about their neighborhoods? Or will they allow prisons to serve their intended function, convincing Hulett and others like him to never harm another human being again?

Works Cited

Hitchens, Peter. "There Is a Way to Beat Crime—Fewer Human Rights, Tougher Prisons, and Admitting That Nothing Deters Killers Like the Death Penalty." Mail on Sunday 30 Mar. 2003: 62.

Lewis, Jean. "Prison: To Punish or to Reform?" PBS P.O.V. 16 Dec. 2003.

Muhlhausen, David. "The Problem with Prisons." Heritage Foundation 4 Feb. 2004. < www.heritage.org >.

Murray, Charles. "Simple Justice." Sunday Times (London) 25 Jan. 2004: 1.

Exercise A: Create an Outline from an Existing Essay

As you did for the first model essay in this section, create an outline that could have been used to write "Heavy Sentences Help America." Be sure to identify the essay's thesis statement, its supporting ideas, and key pieces of evidence that are used.

Exercise B: Create an Outline for an Opposing Cause-and-Effect Essay

The second model essay offers one point of view concerning prisons. For this exercise, your assignment is to find supporting ideas, create an outline, and ultimately write the body of a five-paragraph multiple-effect essay that argues an opposing view. (A later assignment in this book will encourage you to practice writing this essay's introduction and conclusion.)

Part 1: Find Supporting Ideas

Using information from Sections One and Three of this book and your own research, you will write an essay that supports the following thesis statement: Prisons are bad for America.

Use outside research or the material in this book to come up with at least three arguments that illustrate a clear reason why prisons are harmful to inmates or society. Each argument will be presented in its own paragraph and should be expressed in the paragraph's topic sentence.

For each of your ideas, write down facts or information that support it. These could be:
- statistical information
- direct quotations
- anecdotes of past events

Example paragraph topic sentence: Prison conditions are dangerous for inmates.

- State prisons are so overcrowded that they operate at up to 117 percent capacity (David Muhlhausen, Viewpoint One).

- Some corrections officers abuse their power by spying on or groping prisoners, harassing or intimidating inmates, and provoking fights among prisoners (Ralph A. Rossum and Constance Rossum, Viewpoint Three).
- Quote from the Rossums: "So many of the guards regard [prisoners] as objects of gratification, derision, and contempt."

Now come up with two other paragraph topics that support your thesis statement.

Part 2: Place the Information from Part 1 in Outline Form

Thesis statement:

    I. Effect A

        Details and elaboration

    II. Effect B

        Details and elaboration

    III. Effect C

        Details and elaboration

Part 3: Write the Arguments in Paragraph Form

You now have three arguments that support the paragraph's thesis statement as well as supporting material. Use the outline to write your three supporting arguments in paragraph form. Make sure each paragraph has a topic sentence that clearly states the paragraph's thesis. Then, add supporting sentences that express facts, quotes, and examples that support each paragraph's argument. The paragraph may also have a concluding or summary sentence.

Imprisoning Juveniles Reduces Crime

Editor's Notes The essay that follows illustrates the third type of cause-and-effect essay. This type of essay explains multiple sequential causes of a single event or phenomenon. It explains how A causes B, which then causes C, which in turn leads to D. This is known as a chain of events or a domino effect. This type of essay generally explains events chronologically, in the order in which they occurred.

Model Essay Three also differs from the previous model essays in that it is longer than five paragraphs. Sometimes five paragraphs are not enough to adequately develop an idea. Moreover, the ability to sustain an argument throughout a longer research or position paper is a valuable skill. Learning how to develop a longer piece of writing will give you the tools you need to advance academically.

Throughout the essay, the author uses statistics, quotes, and other supporting details to back up the arguments she makes. As you read, use the sidebar questions to identify the essay's thesis statement and learn how the essay is organized.

■ Refers to thesis and topic sentences

■ Refers to supporting details

Paragraph 1

Some criminal rights organizations, religious groups, and parents are calling for special, lenient treatment of juvenile criminals. They claim that sentencing juveniles to time in adult prisons does not deter crime and is too harsh a punishment. Adult prisons, they charge, are frightening, dangerous, and too cruel for youth. However, punishing criminals for their behavior when they are young teaches them to behave better as they grow older. If minors who commit violent crime—such as assault and battery, rape, or murder—are sent to adult jails, they will learn firsthand the consequences of committing crimes and will be less likely to break laws in the future. In fact, a chain of events that

What is the essay's thesis?

began in the 1980s suggests that imprisoning more criminals at a younger age leads to an overall reduction in crime.

Paragraph 2

What is the topic sentence of Paragraph 2?

Juvenile crime rose dramatically from about 1985 to the early 1990s. Shockingly, the number of teenagers arrested for murder nearly tripled during this period, according to the Center on Juvenile and Criminal Justice. Other crimes were also on the rise, with crime committed by juveniles increasing by 60 percent from 1984 to 1998 (Collier C1). Compared to young criminals of the past, these delinquents were more sophisticated and violent. Many were connected to gangs, brandished dangerous weapons during their crimes, and were involved in the growing and increasingly violent crack cocaine markets of inner cities.

Paragraph 3

What authorities are quoted in the essay?

Many of these criminal youths were tried in the juvenile justice system and were sentenced to time in juvenile detention centers. However, these facilities do not punish in the same way as adult prisons. Lawyer Linda J. Collier, who has worked in juvenile courts, asserts, "Detaining a rapist or murderer in a juvenile facility until the age of 18 or 21 isn't even a slap on the hand" (Collier C1). Originally created to protect and help wayward children, the juvenile justice system is better suited for dealing with pranksters and kids who skip school rather than for punishing serious criminals. In this way, juvenile centers coddle young criminals more than they punish them. Columnist and editor Woody

What transitions are used in Paragraph 3?

West maintains, "As a result of what has become a . . . feeble juvenile criminal justice system . . . the young have learned an ominous lesson: they can get away with breaking the law indefinitely with hardly a risk of swift, sure and stern punishment." Making matters worse, juvenile detention centers became so crowded that some violent criminals who should have been locked up were sent home and electronically monitored from there. How does sitting at home watching Jerry Springer and surfing the Internet help young criminals pay society back for their crimes?

Paragraph 4

During this period the news media began to heavily publicize crimes committed by juveniles. They attributed the rising crime rate to an ineffective juvenile justice system. Reporter Jack Kresnak describes how the news media declared a "'juvenile crime epidemic' . . . news reports of kids who seemed to act without remorse or conscience fed the public perception that juvenile courts were unable to deal with this new danger." It became evident that the juvenile justice system could not be relied upon to punish hardened youths who committed adult crimes. Not surprisingly, many citizens and members of Congress clamored for tougher sentencing of minors.

Paragraph 5

In response, in the 1990s nearly every state passed or amended laws that allowed young offenders to be tried and punished in the adult justice system. This meant that juveniles who had committed violent crimes, burglary, and drug offenses could now be sentenced to prison terms with adults. Some states lowered the age at which minors could be tried as adults for certain crimes to as low as ten years old. On the federal level, the Office of Juvenile Justice and Delinquency Prevention (OJJDP) eased restrictions on the cohabitation of juveniles and adults. All of these factors combined to allow harsher punishment of juveniles who ran afoul of the law. After these laws were implemented, the number of minors serving time in adult prisons increased sharply. According to Rimer of the *New York Times*, the number of youths in adult facilities doubled from 1985 to 1998. Many prisons held minors in separate wings, but youths still mixed with adult inmates in cafeterias, libraries, and recreation centers.

> What is the thesis of Paragraph 5?

> From what sources did the author find facts and statistics to back up her argument?

Paragraph 6

Facing the prospect of going to an adult prison—or returning to one—seemed to scare youths straight. Indeed, juvenile arrest rates have decreased since 1994. According to the OJJDP, for the crime of murder, arrest rates decreased 74 percent from 1993 to 2000. Obviously, the message that serious crimes beget harsh consequences worked. The Center on Juvenile and Criminal Justice concludes from crime statistics of the late

> What chain of events has the author chronicled through this paragraph?

1990s, "The youngest teens and children show the largest declines in crime of any age group, foretelling a law abiding coming generation." The facts indicate that imprisoning juvenile criminals led to the current low crime rate.

Paragraph 7

What idea does the author revisit from Paragraph 1?

It is no coincidence that this reduction in crime came on the heels of more punitive juvenile justice measures. Now is certainly not the time to reverse this progress by paying heed to those who would softly handle young criminals. Attorney Kenneth Sukhia warns, "I have seen firsthand the devastating effects of an ineffective juvenile justice system. . . . Juvenile offenders have been taught to believe through repeated brushes with the system that unless they commit murder, they stand little or no chance of being incarcerated for their crimes." Undoubtedly, crime is best suppressed by deterring lawbreakers before they become career criminals. The future of our youth and our society depends on it.

What does Sukhia's quote lend to the essay?

Works Cited

Center on Juvenile and Criminal Justice. "Myths and Facts About Youths and Crime." Accessed on 11 Oct 2006 < www.cjcj.org/jjic/myth_facts.php > .

Collier, Linda J. "Adult Crime, Adult Time: Outdated Juvenile Laws Thwart Justice." Washington Post 29 Mar. 1998: C1.

Kresnak, Jack. "Juvenile Justice." Covering Crime and Justice. Oct. 2005, accessed 11 Oct 2006. Criminal Justice Journalists. < www.justicejournalism.org/crimeguide/chapter02/chapter02_pg05.html > .

Office of Juvenile Justice and Delinquency Prevention. "Juvenile Arrests 2000." Nov. 2002.

Rimer, Sara. "States Adjust Adult Prisons to Needs of Youth Inmates." New York Times 25 July 2001: A1.

Sukhia, Kenneth W. Testimony before the House Subcommittee on Crime, Committee on the Judiciary, 10 Mar 1999, Washington, 1999.

West, Woody. "A Slap on the Wrist for 'Naughty' Kids." Insight 19 Aug. 1996.

Exercise A: Examining Introductions and Conclusions

Every essay features introductory and concluding paragraphs that are used to frame the main ideas presented. Well-written introductions not only present the essay's thesis statement but also capture the reader's attention and make clear why the topic being explored is important. The conclusion reiterates the essay's thesis and is also the last chance for the writer to make an impression on the reader. Strong introductions and conclusions can greatly enhance an essay's impact on an audience.

The Introduction

There are several techniques that can be used to craft an introductory paragraph. An essay can start with:

- an anecdote: a brief story that illustrates a point relevant to the topic.
- startling information: facts or statistics that elucidate the point of the essay.
- setting up and knocking down a position: a position or claim believed by proponents of one side of a controversy, followed by statements that challenge that claim.
- historical perspective: an example of the way things used to be that leads into a discussion of how or why things work differently now.
- summary information: general introductory information about the topic that feeds into the essay's thesis statement.

Remember that in a cause-and-effect essay, the introductory paragraph should establish the cause or the effect that is being examined.

Assignment 1

Reread the introductory paragraphs of the model essays in this section and of the viewpoints in Section One. Identify which of the techniques described above are used in the essays. How else do they grab the attention of the reader? Are their thesis statements clearly presented?

Assignment 2

Write an introduction for the essay you have outlined and partially written in the previous exercise, using one of the techniques described above.

The Conclusion

The conclusion brings the essay to a close by returning to its main ideas. Good conclusions, however, go beyond simply repeating these ideas. Strong conclusions explore a topic's broader implications and reiterate why it is important to consider. They may frame the essay by returning to an anecdote featured in the opening paragraph. Or, they may close with a quotation or refer back to an event in the essay. In opinionated essays, the conclusion should reiterate which side the essay is taking and ask the reader to reconsider a previously held position on the subject.

Assignment 3

Reread the concluding paragraphs of the model essays and of the viewpoints in Section One. Which were most effective in driving their arguments home to the reader? What sorts of techniques did they use to do this? Did they appeal emotionally to the reader or bookend an idea or event referenced elsewhere in the essay?

Assignment 4

Write a conclusion for the essay you have outlined and partially written in the previous exercise using one of the techniques described above.

Writer's Checklist

✔ Review the five-paragraph essay you've written.
✔ Make sure it has a clear introduction that draws the reader in and contains a thesis statement that concisely expresses what your essay is about.
✔ Evaluate the paragraphs and make sure they each have clear topic sentences that are well supported by interesting and relevant details.
✔ Check that you have used compelling and authoritative quotes to enliven the essay.
✔ Finally, be sure you have a solid conclusion that uses one of the techniques presented in this exercise.

Exercise B: Using Quotations to Enliven Your Essay

No essay is complete without quotations. Get in the habit of using quotes to support at least some of the ideas in your essays. Although quotes do not need to appear in every paragraph, there should be enough quotes so that the essay contains voices aside from your own. When you write, use quotations to accomplish the following:

- provide expert advice that you are not necessarily in the position to know about
- cite lively or passionate passages
- include a particularly well-written point that gets to the heart of the matter
- supply statistics or facts that have been derived from someone's research
- deliver anecdotes that illustrate the point you are trying to make
- express first-person testimony

There are some important things to remember when using quotations:

- Note your sources' qualifications and biases. This way your reader can identify the person you have quoted and can put their words in context.
- Put any quoted material within proper quotation marks. Failing to attribute quotes to their authors constitutes plagiarism, which is when an author takes someone else's words or ideas and presents them as their own. Plagiarism is a very serious infraction and must be avoided at all costs.

Assignment 1. Reread the essays presented in all sections of this book and find at least one example of each of the above quotation types.

Write Your Own Five-Paragraph Cause-and-Effect Essay

Using the information from this book, write your own five-paragraph cause-and-effect essay about prisons. The following steps are suggestions on how to get started.

Step One: Choose your topic.

Think carefully before deciding what topic to write about in your cause-and-effect essay. Is there any subject that particularly fascinates you? Is there an issue you strongly support or feel strongly against? Is there a topic you would like to learn more about? Ask yourself such questions before selecting your essay topic. Refer to Appendix D, "Sample Essay Topics," if you need help selecting a topic.

Step Two: Write down questions and answers about the topic.

Before you begin writing, you will need to think carefully about what ideas your essay will contain. This process is known as brainstorming. Brainstorming involves asking yourself questions and coming up with ideas to discuss in your essay. Possible questions that will help you with the brainstorming process include:

- Why is this topic important?
- Why should people be interested in this topic?
- How can I make this essay interesting to the reader?
- What question am I going to address in this paragraph or essay?
- What facts, ideas, or quotes can I use to support the answer to my question?
- Will the question's answer reveal a preference for one subject over another?

Questions especially for cause-and-effect essays include:

- What are the causes of the topic being examined?
- What are the effects of the topic being examined?

- Are there single or multiple causes?
- Are there single or multiple effects?
- Is a chain of events involved?

Step Three: Gather facts and ideas related to your topic.
This book contains several places to find information, including the viewpoints and the appendixes. In addition, you may want to research the books, articles, and Web sites listed in Section Three or do additional research in your local library.

Step Four: Develop a workable thesis statement.
Use what you have written down in Steps Two and Three to help you articulate the main point or argument you want to make in your essay. It should be expressed in a clear sentence and make an arguable or supportable point.

> *Examples:*
>
> **Imprisoning juveniles in adult prisons benefits society.**
> This could be a multiple-effect essay that examines how jailing minors in adult facilities would affect communities.
>
> **Prison reforms can reduce crime.**
> This could be a multiple-cause essay that discusses various ways prisons could be reformed so that fewer released inmates reoffend.

Step Five: Write an outline or diagram.
1. Write the thesis statement at the top of the outline.
2. Write roman numerals I, II, and III on the left side of the page with A, B, and C under each numeral.
3. Next to each roman numeral, write your best ideas from Step Three. These should all directly relate to and support the thesis statement.

4. Next to each letter, write information that supports that particular idea.

Step Six: Write the three supporting paragraphs.
Use your outline to write the three supporting paragraphs. Write down the main idea of each paragraph in sentence form. Do the same thing for the supporting points of information. Each sentence should support the topic of the paragraph. Be sure you have relevant and interesting details, facts, and quotes. Use transitions when you move from idea to idea to keep the text fluid. Sometimes, although not always, paragraphs can include a concluding or summary sentence that restates the paragraph's argument.

Step Seven: Write the introduction and conclusion.
See the previous exercise for information on writing introductions and conclusions.

Step Eight: Read and rewrite.
As you read, check your essay for the following:

✔ Does the essay maintain a consistent tone?
✔ Do all sentences serve to reinforce your general thesis or your paragraph theses?
✔ Do all paragraphs flow from one to the other? Do you need to add transition words or phrases?
✔ Have you quoted from reliable, authoritative, and interesting sources?
✔ Is there a sense of progression throughout the essay?
✔ Does the essay get bogged down in too much detail or irrelevant material?
✔ Does your introduction grab the reader's attention?
✔ Does your conclusion reflect back on any previously discussed material or give the essay a sense of closure?
✔ Are there any spelling or grammatical errors?

Tips on Writing Effective Cause-and-Effect Essays

- You do not need to describe every possible cause of an event or phenomenon. Focus on the most important ones that support your thesis statement.
- Vary your sentence structure. Avoid repeating yourself.
- Maintain a professional, objective tone. Avoid sounding uncertain or insulting.
- Anticipate what the reader's counterarguments may be and answer them.
- Use sources that state facts and evidence.
- Avoid assumptions or generalizations without evidence.
- Avoid writing in the first person.
- Aim for clear, fluid, well-written sentences that together make up an essay that is informative, interesting, and memorable.

**Section Three:
Supporting
Research
Material**

Facts About Prisons

Editor's Note: These facts can be used in reports or papers to reinforce or add credibility when making important points or claims.

Facts About Prisons

- Since 1980 America's prison population has quadrupled to more than 2 million inmates.
- The state and federal prison population grew by more than twenty-eight thousand inmates (1.9 percent) between 2003 and 2004, and the jail population increased by more than twenty-two thousand inmates (3.3 percent).
- As of 2004, 1 out of every 138 Americans was incarcerated in prison or jail.
- Approximately 6.9 million Americans are incarcerated or on probation or parole, an increase of more than 275 percent since 1980.
- A 2002 Bureau of Justice Statistics report states that most state and federal prisons operate beyond 100 percent capacity.
- The incarceration of an inmate costs taxpayers approximately twenty-two thousand dollars per year.
- In California fifty inmates die each year as a result of lack of adequate medical care.
- In 2004 more than one hundred thousand inmates were released from prisons.

Facts About Inmates

According to the Bureau of Justice Statistics:

- Ninety-three percent of prison inmates are male, 7 percent are female.
- As of 2004 more than 190,000 women were serving time in state and federal prisons or local jails.

- Forty-one percent of prison inmates in 2004 were black and 19 percent were Hispanic.
- One in four jail inmates in 2002 was in jail for a drug offense, compared to one in ten in 1983; drug offenders constituted 20 percent of state prison inmates and 55 percent of federal prison inmates in 2001.
- Black males have a 32 percent chance of serving time in prison at some point in their lives; Hispanic males have a 17 percent chance; white males have a 6 percent chance.

Facts About Juveniles and Prisons

- Between 1985 and 1997 the number of juveniles housed in adult state prisons rose from thirty-four hundred to seventy-four hundred. By 1998 more than eleven thousand minors were housed in adult correctional facilities.
- The majority of states allow fourteen-year-olds to be tried as adults.
- Two states, Kansas and Vermont, can try ten-year-olds as adults.
- Twenty-three states have no minimum age for minors to be tried as adults.
- The United Nations Convention on the Rights of the Child, an international treaty that the United States has not signed, forbids sentencing any minor with life imprisonment without parole.

Prisons Around the World

According to the International Centre for Prison Studies:
- More than 9 million people are held in penal institutions throughout the world. Almost half of these are in the United States (2.09 million), China (1.55 million), and Russia (0.76 million).
- The United States has the highest prison-population rate in the world, some 714 per 100,000 of the national population.

- Belarus, Bermuda, and Russia have the next highest rate, 532 per 100,000 of the national population.
- The nations with the next highest rates of incarceration are Palau (523 per 100,000), the U.S. Virgin Islands (490), Turkmenistan (489), Cuba (487), Suriname (437), the Cayman Islands (429), Belize (420), the Ukraine (417), the Maldive Islands (416), St. Kitts and Nevis (415), South Africa (413), and the Bahamas (410).
- Almost three-fifths of all countries (58 percent) have rates below 150 per 100,000.

Facts About Prison Recidivism

In 2002 the Justice Department's Bureau of Justice Statistics conducted the largest recidivism study in U.S. history. Its findings included the following facts:

- Sixty-seven percent of inmates released from state prisons in 1994 committed at least one serious new crime within the following three years.
- State prisoners with the highest rearrest rates were those who had been incarcerated for stealing motor vehicles (79 percent), possessing or selling stolen property (77 percent), larceny (75 percent), burglary (74 percent), robbery (70 percent), or those using, possessing, or trafficking in illegal weapons (70 percent).
- Those with the lowest rearrest rates were former inmates who had been in prison for homicide (41 percent), sexual assault (41 percent), rape (46 percent), or driving under the influence of drugs or alcohol (51 percent).
- About 1 percent of released prisoners who had served time for murder were arrested for another homicide within three years, and about 2 percent of rapists were arrested for another rape within three years.
- Within three years 52 percent of released prisoners were back in prison either because of a new crime or because they had violated their parole conditions

(for example, they had failed a drug test or missed a parole-office appointment).

- Men are more likely to be rearrested than are women (68 percent, compared to 58 percent).
- Blacks are more likely to be rearrested than whites (73 percent vs. 63 percent).
- Non-Hispanics are more likely to be rearrested than Hispanics (71 percent vs. 65 percent).
- Younger prisoners and those with longer records are more likely to be rearrested than older prisoners and those with shorter records.
- Almost 8 percent of all released prisoners were rearrested for a new crime in a state other than the one that released them.
- Most former convicts were rearrested shortly after getting out of prison: 30 percent within six months, 44 percent within a year, 59 percent within two years, and 67 percent by the end of three years.

Finding and Using Sources of Information

No matter what type of essay you are writing, it is necessary to find information to support your point of view. You can use sources such as books as well as magazine, newspaper, and online articles.

Using Books and Articles

You can find books and articles in a library by using the library's computer or cataloging system. If you are not sure how to use these resources, ask a librarian to help you. You can also use a computer to find many magazine articles and other articles written specifically for the Internet.

You are likely to find a lot more information than you can possibly use in your essay, so your first task is to narrow it down to what is likely to be most usable. Look at book and article titles. Look at book chapter titles and examine the book's index to see if it contains information on your chosen topic. For example, if you want to write about prisons reducing crime and you find a book about crime, check the chapter titles and index to be sure it contains information about prisons reducing crime before you bother to check out the book.

For a five-paragraph essay, you do not need a great deal of supporting information, so quickly try to narrow down your materials to a few good books and magazine or Internet articles. You do not need dozens. You might even find that two good books or articles contain all the information you need.

You probably do not have time to read an entire book, so skim the chapters or sections that relate to your topic. When you find useful information, copy it onto a note-card or notebook. You should look for supporting facts, statistics, quotations, and examples.

Using the Internet

When you select your supporting information, it is important that you evaluate its source. This is especially important with information you find on the Internet. Because nearly anyone can put information on the Internet, there is as much bad information as good information. Before using Internet information—or any information—try to determine if the source seems reliable. Is the author or Internet site sponsored by a legitimate organization? Is it from a government source? Does the author have any special knowledge or training related to the topic? Does the article give any indication of the information's origin?

Using Your Supporting Information

When you use supporting information from a book, article, interview, or other source, there are three important things to remember:

1. *Make it clear whether you are using a direct quotation or a paraphrase.* If you copy information directly from your source, you are quoting it. You must put quotation marks around the information and credit the source. If you put the information in your own words, you are paraphrasing it.

   Here is an example of a using a quotation:
   Writer Jim Holt questions the validity of punishing criminals. He believes brain damage has made many of them incapable of controlling their violent urges: "Because of damage to the frontal lobes of their brains caused by birth complications, accidents or brutal childhood beatings, they simply can't contain their aggressive impulses; compared with the rest of us, they live life on a neurological hair trigger. Clearly, society needs to protect itself from these people. But does it need to punish them?" (Holt 21).

Here is an example of a brief paraphrase of the same passage:

Author Jim Holt questions the validity of punishing criminals. He claims that many violent criminals have suffered brain damage that makes them incapable of controlling their aggression. He wonders whether it is necessary to punish criminals who truly cannot control their violent tendencies.

2. *Use the information fairly.* Be careful to use supporting information in the way the author intended it. For example, it is unfair to quote an author as saying, "Prisons reduce crime" when he or she said, "Prisons reduce crime no more than they reduce violence—and they continue to be brutally violent places." This is called taking information out of context. This is using supporting evidence unfairly.

3. *Give credit where credit is due.* Giving credit is known as citing. You must use citations when you use someone else's information, but not every piece of supporting information needs a citation.
   - If the supporting information is general knowledge—that is, it can be found in many sources— you do not have to cite your source.
   - If you directly quote a source, you must cite it.
   - If you paraphrase information from a specific source, you must cite it.

If you do not use citations where you should, you are plagiarizing—or stealing—someone else's work.

Citing Your Sources

There are a number of ways to cite your sources. Your teacher will probably want you to do it in one of three ways:
   - Informal: As in the examples in number 1 above, you tell where you found the information in the same place that you use it.
   - Informal list: At the end of the article, place an unnumbered list of the sources you used. This

tells the reader where, in general, you found your information.

- Formal: Use a formal citation, as in the first example in number 1. A list of works cited is generally placed at the end of an article or essay, although it may be located in different places depending on your teacher's requirements. An example of an endnote follows:

Work Cited

Holt, Jim. "Decarcerate?" <u>New York Times Magazine</u> 15 Aug. 2004: 20–21.

Using MLA Style to Create a Works Cited List

You will probably need to create a list of works cited for your paper. A Works Cited list includes materials that you quoted from, paraphrased, or summarized. When you also include other works you consulted in your research, call this section Works Consulted. There are several different ways to structure these references. The following examples are based on the Modern Language Association (MLA) style, one of the major citation styles used by writers.

Book Entries

For most book entries you will need the author's name, the book's title, where it was published, what company published it, and the year it was published. This information is usually found on the inside of the book. Variations on book entries include the following:

A book by a single author:
Guest, Emma. Children of AIDS: Africa's Orphan Crisis. London: Sterling, 2003.

Two or more books by the same author:
Friedman, Thomas L. From Beirut to Jerusalem. New York: Doubleday, 1989.

---. The World Is Flat: A Brief History of the Twentieth Century. New York: Farrar, 2005.

A book by two or more authors:
Pojman, Louis P., and Jeffrey Reiman. The Death Penalty: For and Against. Lanham: Rowman, 1998.

A book with an editor:
Friedman, Lauri S., ed. At Issue: What Motivates Suicide Bombers? San Diego: Greenhaven, 2004.

Periodical and Newspaper Entries

Entries for sources found in periodicals and newspapers are cited a bit differently than books. These sources usually have a title and a publication name. They also may have specific dates and page numbers. Unlike book entries, you do not need to list where newspapers or periodicals are published or what company publishes them.

An article from a periodical:
Snow, Keith Harmon. "State Terror in Ethiopia." <u>Z Magazine</u> June 2004: 33–35.

An article from a newspaper:
Constantino, Rebecca. "Fostering Love, Respecting Race." <u>Los Angeles Times</u> 14 Dec. 2002: B17.

Internet Sources

To document a source you find online, provide as much information as possible, including the author's name, the title of the document, the date of publication or of last revision, your date of access, and the URL (enclosed in brackets).

A Web source:
Shyovitz, David. "The History and Development of Yiddish." <u>Jewish Virtual Library</u>. 30 May 2005. <www.jewishvirtuallibrary.org/jsource/History/yiddish.html>.

Your teacher will tell you exactly how information should be cited in your essay. Generally, the very least information needed is the original author's name and the name of the article or other publication, and the URL of the page you are citing.

Be sure you know exactly what information your teacher requires before you start looking for your supporting information so that you know what information to record in your notes.

Sample Essay Topics

Cause-and-Effect Essays

Prisons deter crime

Prisons do not deter crime

Prisons protect the public from violence

Prisons increase violence

Prison labor helps rehabilitate inmates

Prison labor exploits inmates

Drug courts more effectively reduce crime than prison

Drug courts are not effective alternatives to prison

Many factors affect whether a convict can be rehabilitated while in prison

Many factors caused juvenile crime to decrease in the late 1990s

Implementing harsher prison sentencing laws would imprison too many people

The war on drugs causes prison overcrowding

General Persuasive Essays

Prisons should focus on punishment

Prisons should focus on rehabilitation

Juveniles should be sent to adult prisons

Juveniles should not be sent to adult prisons

Prisons abuse inmates

Prisons do not abuse inmates

Prisons should be segregated by race

Prisons should not be segregated by race

Alternatives to prison should be pursued

Prison alternatives should not be pursued

Prisons should be reformed

Prisons do not need reform

Supermaximun-security prisons violate human rights

Supermaximum-security prisons are necessary

Organizations to Contact

American Civil Liberties Union (ACLU)
1875 Connecticut Ave. NW, Suite 410, Washington, DC 20009
(202) 234-4830 • e-mail: aclu@aclu.org • Web site:
www.aclu.org

The ACLU works to defend civil liberties. It maintains a
national prisons resource center and litigates cases to
strengthen and protect adult and juvenile offenders' Eighth
Amendment rights.

American Correctional Association (ACA)
4380 Forbes Blvd., Lanham, MD 20706-4322 • (800) 222-5646
• e-mail: harryw@aca.org • Web site: www.corrections.com

The ACA is committed to improving national and international correctional policy and to promoting the professional development of those working in the field of corrections.

Amnesty International
322 Eighth Ave., New York, NY 10001 • (212) 807-8400
Web site: www.amnesty-usa.org

Amnesty International is an independent worldwide movement working impartially for the release of all prisoners
of conscience, fair and prompt trials for political prisoners, and an end to torture and executions.

Campaign for an Effective Crime Policy
918 F St. NW, Suite 505, Washington, DC 20004 • (202)
628-1903 • e-mail: info@crimepolicy.com

Launched in 1992 by a group of criminal justice leaders,
the nonpartisan Campaign for an Effective Crime Policy
advocates alternative-sentencing policies. It also works
to educate the public about the relative effectiveness of
various strategies for improving public safety.

Cato Institute

1000 Massachusetts Ave. NW, Washington, DC 20001-5403
(202) 842-0200 • e-mail: cato@cato.org • Web site:
www.cato.org

The institute is a libertarian public policy research foundation dedicated to limiting the role of government and protecting individual liberties. The institute evaluates government policies and offers reform proposals in its publication *Policy Analysis*.

Families Against Mandatory Minimums (FAMM)

1612 K St. NW, Suite 1400, Washington, DC 20006 • (202) 822-6700 • e-mail: famm@famm.org • Web site: www.famm.org

FAMM is an educational organization that works to repeal mandatory-minimum prison sentences. It provides legislators, the public, and the media with information on and analyses of minimum-sentencing laws.

Heritage Foundation

214 Massachusetts Ave. NE, Washington, DC 20002 • (202) 546-4400 • e-mail: pubs@heritage.org • Web site: www. heritage.org

The Heritage Foundation is a conservative public policy research institute. It is a proponent of limited government and advocates tougher sentencing and the construction of more prisons.

National Center for Policy Analysis (NCPA)

655 15th St. NW, Suite 375, Washington, DC 20005 • (202) 628-6671 • e-mail: ncpa@public-policy.org • Web site: www.ncpa.org

The NCPA is a nonprofit public policy research institute. It advocates more stringent prison sentences, the abolishment of parole, and restitution for crimes.

National Center on Institutions and Alternatives (NCIA)

635 Slaters Lane, Suite G-100, Alexandria, VA 22314 • (703) 684-0373 • Web site: www.ncianet.org

The NCIA is a criminal justice foundation that encourages community-based alternatives to prison that are more effective in providing education, training, and personal skills required for the rehabilitation of nonviolent offenders. The center advocates doubling "good conduct" credit for the early release of nonviolent first-time offenders in the federal system to make room for violent offenders.

Police Foundation

1201 Connecticut Ave. NW, Washington, DC 20036 • (202) 833-1460 • e-mail: pfinfo@policefoundation.org • Web site: www.policefoundation.org

The Police Foundation is committed to increasing police effectiveness in controlling crime, maintaining order, and providing humane and efficient service. The foundation sponsors forums that debate and disseminate ideas to improve personnel and practice in American criminal policing.

Sentencing Project

918 F St. NW, Suite 501, Washington, DC 20004 • (202) 628-0871 • e-mail: staff@sentencingproject.org • Web site: www.sentencingproject.org

The project seeks to provide public defenders and other public officials with information on establishing and improving alternative-sentencing programs that provide convicted persons with positive and constructive options to incarceration. It promotes increased public understanding of the sentencing process and alternative-sentencing programs.

U.S. Department of Justice
Federal Bureau of Prisons

320 First St. NW, Washington, DC 20534 • e-mail: web master@bop.gov • Web site: www.bop.gov

The Federal Bureau of Prisons works to protect society by confining offenders in the controlled environments of prisons and community-based facilities. It believes in providing work and other self-improvement opportunities within these facilities to assist offenders in becoming law-abiding citizens.

Bibliography

Books

Abramsky, Sasha, *Hard Time Blues: How Politics Built a Prison Nation.* New York: Thomas Dunne, 2002.

Bosworth, Mary, ed., *Encyclopedia of Prisons and Correctional Facilities.* Thousand Oaks, CA: Sage, 2005.

Butts, Jeffrey, and John Roman, eds., *Juvenile Drug Courts and Teen Substance Abuse.* Washington, DC: Urban Institute, 2004.

Elsner, Alan, *Gates of Injustice: The Crisis of America's Prisons.* Princeton, NJ: Prentice Hall, 2004.

Hanrahan, Clare, ed., *Opposing Viewpoints: America's Prisons.* Detroit: Greenhaven/Thomson Gale, 2006.

Myers, David L., *Boys Among Men: Trying and Sentencing Juveniles as Adults.* Westport, CT: Praeger, 2005.

Pollock, Joycelyn M., *Prisons and Prison Life: Costs and Consequences.* Los Angeles: Roxbury, 2004.

Prisons Foundation, *Prisons Almanac 2005.* Washington, DC: Prisons Foundation, 2005.

Rabiger, Joanna, *Daily Prison Life.* Broomall, PA: Mason Crest, 2003.

Tabarrok, Alexander, ed., *Changing the Guard: Private Prisons and the Control of Crime.* Oakland, CA: Independent Institute, 2003.

Travis, Jeremy, and Michelle Waul, eds., *Prisoners Once Removed: The Impact of Incarceration and Reentry on Children, Families, and Communities.* Washington, DC: Urban Institute, 2003.

Williams, Stanley "Tookie," and Barbara Cottman Becnel, *Life in Prison.* New York: SeaStar, 2001.

Periodicals

Aborn, Richard M., "Time to End Recidivism," *Nation,* March 9, 2005.

Allen, Norm R., "Reforming the Incarceration Nation," *Free Inquiry,* Summer 2001.

Bierma, Nathan, "Doing Time: Do Correctional Facilities Correct Anything?" *Books & Culture,* January/February 2004.

Carter, Marcia J., and Kelly J. Russell, "What Is the Perceived Worth of Recreation? Results from a County Jail Study," *Corrections Today,* June 2005.

DiIulio, John J. Jr., and Joseph P. Tierney, "An Easy Ride for Felons on Probation," *New York Times,* August 29, 2000.

Hurd, Douglas, "Does Prison Really Work?" *Spectator,* May 14, 2005.

Jacoby, Jeff, "More Prisoners, Less Crime," *Boston Globe.* August 28, 2003.

Koch, Edward I., "Harsh Punishments Curb Crime," *NewsMax,* April 28, 2005.

Krisberg, Barry, "A Case Against Mass Incarceration," *Los Angeles Times,* January 18, 2005.

Lehrer, Eli, "Justice Behind Bars: Getting Back to Our Own Prison Problem," *National Review,* June 14, 2004.

Lockwood, Michael, and Rachel Alexander, "What's Really Happening in Sheriff Joe Arpaio's Jail," *Intellectual Conservative,* March 25, 2002.

Lowry, Richard, "Prisons Keep Crime Rate Down," *Conservative Chronicle,* September 18, 2002.

Marciniak, Ed, "Standing Room Only: What to Do About Prison Overcrowding," *Commonweal,* January 25, 2002.

Marks, Alexandra, "Prisons Review Results from 'Get-Tough' Era: The Number of Convicted Felons Serving Life Sentences Has Increased 83 percent, but Crime Is Down by 35 Percent," *Christian Science Monitor,* May 12, 2004.

Mathis, Greg, "Alternative Sentencing Can Reduce Prison Population," *Call & Post,* May 12–18, 2005.

Neumayr, George, "Crime and No Punishment," *American Spectator,* July 9, 2003.

Russell, Malik, "The Misperceptions of Three Strikes Laws," *National Bar Association Magazine*, September–December 2004.

Snyder, Leslie Crocker, "Reform the Reforms," *New York Times,* January 8, 2006.

Talbot, Margaret, "Catch and Release," *Atlantic Monthly,* January/February 2003.

Twohey, Megan, "The Wrong Answer to Littleton," *Washington Monthly,* June 1999.

Van Wormer, Katherine, "Restoring Justice," *USA Today Magazine,* November 2001.

Westerman, Ted, "Three-Strikes Law Does Serve the State Well," *Los Angeles Times,* September 28, 1999.

Internet Sources

Backstrom, James C., "A Common Sense Approach to Housing Juvenile Offenders in Adult Detention Facilities," Dakota County Attorney's Office, 2000. www.co.dakota.mn.us.

Ensign, John, statement before the U.S. Senate on the Mandatory Prisoner Work and Drug Testing Act of 2003, Washington, DC, March 20, 2003. http://ensign.senate.gov.

Fine, Glenn A., "Statement Before the Commission on Safety and Abuse in America's Prisons," April 19, 2005. www.usdoj.gov.

Gainsborough, Jenni, "The Truth About Private Prisons," AlterNet.org, December 15, 2003. www.alternet.org.

Heilig, Steve, and David E. Smith, "Arresting the Jail Juggernaut: Drug Treatment Instead of Imprisonment," San Francisco Medical Society, 2005. www.sfms.org.

Janda, John, "The Mind of the Parolee: A View from the Trenches," *Friends Committee on Legislation Newsletter,* August/September 2004. www.fclca.org.

Levick, Marsha, and Paul Pfingst, hosted by Margaret Warner, PBS Online NewsHour, July 26, 2001. www.pbs.org.

Markos, Kibret, "Prison Reform Idea: Make Worst Inmates Suffer," NorthJersey.com, July 3, 2005. www.north jersey.com.

National Center for Policy Analysis, "Does Punishment Deter?" NCPA Policy Backgrounder 148, August 17, 1998. www.ncpa.org.

Index

Picture Credits

About the Editor

Jamuna Carroll is a writer, an editor, and a poet who holds a bachelor's degree in writing and mass communication. She has compiled nine anthologies, most of which center on civil liberties issues.